An Exhortation to Resolve Upon Bodhi

An Exhortation to Resolve Upon Bodhi

with commentary by

Venerable Master Hsuan Hua

English translation by the
Buddhist Text Translation Society

Buddhist Text Translation Society
Dharma Realm Buddhist University
Dharma Realm Buddhist Association
Burlingame, California U.S.A

An Exhortation to Resolve Upon Bodhi
The ultimate committment of a Buddhist

Published and translated by:

Buddhist Text Translation Society
1777 Murchison Drive, Burlingame, CA 94010-4504

First edition 2003

12 11 10 09 08 07 06 05 04 03 10 09 08 07 06 05 04 03 02 01

ISBN 0-88139-424-6

Printed in Malaysia.

Addresses of the Dharma Realm Buddhist Association branches are
listed at the back of this book.

Library of Congress Cataloging-in-Publication Data

Shixian, 1686-1734.
  [Quan fa pu ti xin wen. English]
  An exhortation to resolve upon bodhi : the ultimate committment of a
buddhist / By Great Master Sying An ; with commentary by Venerable
Master Hsuan Hua ; English translation by the Buddhist Text Translation
Society.
      p. cm.
  ISBN 0-88139-424-6
1. Bodhicitta (Buddhism) I. Hsüan Hua, 1908- II. Buddhist Text
Translation Society. III. Title.

  BQ4398.5.S5513 2003
  294.3'444--dc21

                                                      2003004474

Contents

Brief Briography of Great Master Sying An

The Master's name was Shr Syan, "Real Sage." His formal name was Sz Chi, "Wanting to Equal," and his style name was Sying An, "Reflection and Sanctuary."

He was the son of the Shr family from the Chang Shou District. His parents raised him in the Confucian tradition. He left home at an early age and practiced the Vinaya (moral precepts) very strictly. He always enjoyed listening to the Dharma. His knowledge of the teachings was profound, and included both the School of the Nature and the School of Marks. He investigated the topic "who is mindful of the Buddha" when he meditated. He concentrated without cease for over four months and suddenly achieved enlightenment. He said, "I have awakened from a dream!"

Ever after, his skillful instructions in the style of the Chan School were both quick and sharp. His eloquence was compelling and invincible.

The Master studied the Tripitaka by day and recited the Buddha's name by night. He burned his finger as a sacrifice before the Buddhas at Ashoka (Mountain) Monastery and made forty-eight great vows. His sincerity elicited a response from the Buddha's sharira, and they put forth splendorous light.

An essay he wrote called "An Exhortation to Resolve Upon Bodhi" encouraged the four-fold assembly in their cultivation. Many of the people who read this essay were moved to tears.

On the fourteenth day of the fourth lunar month during the twelfth year of the Yung Jeng reign period (A.D. 1734 of the Ching Dynasty), he faced West and quietly passed away.

Myriads of people attended the funeral of Great Master Sying An. Suddenly he opened his eyes and said, "I am going now and will come back soon. Birth and death are the important matter. Everyone should purify his mind and recite the Buddha's name to end birth and death."

He put his palms together and recited the Buddha's name continuously, then passed away once again. A verse of praise goes:

His compassionate mind was so vast that he wrote an essay called "An Exhortation to Resolve Upon Bodhi."

His vow power was so profound that he made forty-eight vows in all.

His practice and understanding of Buddhism were so real and true that his auspicious responses were beyond compare.

Therefore, the lineage of the Pure Land School survives due to his strenuous efforts.

The Venerable Master Hsuan Hua

Eight Aspects of a Resolve

Essay:

I, the unworthy Shr Syan, a lowly, ordinary Sanghan, weeping blood and bowing to the ground, exhort the great assembly and present-day men and women of pure faith: please listen and consider what I am about to say.

We have heard that resolving the mind is foremost among the essential doors for entering the Path, and that making vows is first among the crucial matters in cultivation. By making vows, we can save living beings. By resolving our minds, we can realize the Buddhas' Path. If we do not make our resolve great and our vows firm, we will remain on the turning wheel throughout as many kalpas as there are particles of dust. Any cultivation will be only bitter toil done in vain.

As the *Flower Adornment Sutra* says, "If you forget your resolve upon Bodhi, your cultivation of even wholesome practices becomes the karma of demons." From this it is clear that forgetting our resolve upon Bodhi is even worse than having never made the resolve.

Thus we know that anyone wishing to study the vehicle of the Thus Come Ones must first make the vows of a Bodhisattva without delay.

Commentary:

An Exhortation to Resolve Upon Bodhi. This essay is a series of logical reasons for encouraging us to make a resolve. What resolve should we make? We should resolve upon Bodhi.

What is the resolve upon Bodhi? It is a resolve to understand. It is the resolve to turn back from confusion and return to enlightenment, to give up what is deviant and return to what is proper, to clearly know right from wrong, to stop being upside-down, and to be straightforward. There is absolutely nothing devious or crooked about a straightforward mind. The resolve for Bodhi is a resolve to benefit people. By benefiting others, you yourself benefit. By working to lead others to become enlightened, you yourself become enlightened.

"Bodhi" is a Sanskrit term. It means "to enlighten to the Path." You understand the Path, and thus are able to cultivate. You can't cultivate if you don't understand the Path; you will be upsidedown forever. You'll think what is right is wrong and what is wrong is right. You'll think black is white and get everything backwards.

You'll walk the proper road if you understand the Path. If not, you'll walk a deviant path. The important point of resolving on Bodhi is that you do no evil, but respectfully practice all good. These are simply the moral precepts. You maintain your resolve for Bodhi if you follow the rules. You have forgotten your resolve when you don't follow the rules.

By Shramana Shr Syan of the Brahma Heaven Monastery in Ancient Hangzhou. From of old, the area has been called Hangzhou. Hangzhou has been a place where the Buddhadharma has flourished. In the past, the Seven Buddhas of Antiquity had come into this world in different places in Hangzhou such as Tian Tai Mountain, Northern View Mountain, Western View Mountain, Southern View Mountain, and Eastern View Mountain. The people of China have deep roots in the Great Vehicle because the Buddhas of the past have chosen to come into this world in China, thus the seeds were planted very early on.

"Brahma Heaven Monastery." "Brahma" means "pure." The Brahma Heaven is a heaven of purity. "Shramana" is an ordinary title of left-home people. It is Sanskrit and means "to diligently wipe out." You "diligently cultivate precepts, samadhi, and wisdom," meaning that you aren't upside-down, and it also means "to wipe out greed, hatred, and stupidity," meaning that you aren't muddled or ignorant. It is a title for all fully-ordained monastics; the person specifically referred to here is Shr Syan. His other name is Sz Chi. His other title is Sying An, the title most people use; therefore, the title page lists this name of the Great Master as author.

It is called an essay because of the style in which it was written. It has an introduction, body, and conclusion. The many doctrines are succinctly stated paragraph by paragraph. And the Master used the appropriate outline, grammar, and particles for the style. It is terse, yet the ideas are stated in full. Thus this essay is very important.

The Master begins: **I, the unworthy Shr Syan, a lowly, ordinary Sanghan.** He was genuinely sincere at this point. His sincerity showed because he was **weeping blood.** He wept until his eyes bled. Think this over: if not for his sincerity, how else could he have cried until he wept tears of blood? Although this is just a figure of speech, it is used to show his sincerity. **And bowing to the ground,** in a full prostration, he was about to **exhort the great assembly,** which includes all monastics and lay people, and all other living beings. "Great assembly" refers to many kinds of living beings, not simply humans alone. **And present-day men and women of pure faith,** the present-day then, and the present day now, referring to the pure and faithful men and women then and now, including both monastic and lay disciples. **Please** kindly **listen and consider what I am about to say.** Now I hope you all will be kind and spare a few moments to listen to and think over what I have to say.

We have heard people say **that resolving the mind is foremost among the essential doors for entering the Path.** We definitely must resolve on Bodhi; it is the most important step. **And that making vows is first among the crucial matters in cultivation.** What is the most crucial part of cultivating that we must understand? Making vows. We absolutely must make vows or else we'll be unable to cultivate. Our attempts will be making pretenses at cultivating the Path. Not daring to make vows, what Path will we be cultivating? We'll be cheating people. If we really want to cultivate the Path, why wouldn't we dare to make vows? "Making vows is first among the crucial matters in cultivation." **By making vows, we can save living beings.** Our vows support us. Without vows, people may even say that they cultivate, but will forget at crucial moments, and not remember what they have said. The power of our vows will be like a boat with which we can ferry people across. How can we ferry anyone across without a boat? **By resolving our minds, we can realize the Buddhas' Path.** By resolving on Bodhi, we will have what it takes to become a Buddha. People don't create the opportunity to become Buddhas unless they resolve on Bodhi. This is the crux, the important message. **If we do not make our resolve great,** if we fail to make a great resolve, we may instead become petty and narrow-minded, unable to take even the slightest loss or renounce anything. We should make **our vows firm** and unchanging; I will do what I said without fail. Otherwise, **we will remain on the turning wheel throughout as many kalpas as there are particles of dust.** Such people will never be able to cease traversing through the turning wheel of the six paths: the three good paths of the gods, the humans, the asuras, and the three evil paths of the hells, the hungry ghosts, and the animals. We'll keep touring the circuit. By doing good deeds, we may be reborn as a god in the heavens or as a person in the world and live a life of luxury. But what is the point of such a life? We "remain on the turning wheel." **Any cultivation,** being vegetarian, reciting sutras, reciting the Buddha's name, **will be only bitter toil done in vain.** Without the resolve for Bodhi, no matter how much we do, it will only be a lot of hard work without any ultimate results; any practices we do will not be ultimate.

As the *Flower Adornment Sutra* says, **"If you forget your resolve upon Bodhi, your cultivation of even wholesome practices becomes the karma of demons."** We will end up doing the deeds of heavenly demons, because we have failed to sever ignorance. We may cultivate, but if we have forgotten our resolve on Bodhi, our mindfulness will be impure. When our mindfulness is pure, we are supported by the resolve for Bodhi. When our mindfulness is impure, we will create the karma of demons. **From this it is clear that forgetting our resolve upon Bodhi** may cause us to create demonic karma even when cultivating wholesome practices. That **is even worse than having never made the resolve.** What will we be cultivating if you don't resolve on Bodhi? It's to be feared that anything we cultivate will be demonic karma.

Thus we know that anyone wishing to study the vehicle of the Thus Come Ones, the Buddhadharma, **must first make the vows of a Bodhisattva.** We must have the resolve of the Bodhi-sattva. Without the vow-power of a Bodhisattva, we will get stuck in the demons' lair. **Without delay,** don't wait to resolve on Bodhi. You may not say, "Wait a while, then I'll resolve on Bodhi and make the vows of a Bodhisattva." You certainly must make the resolve for Bodhi and vow to cultivate the Bodhisattva path; then, you can transcend the turning wheel and end birth and death.

Essay:

But resolves and vows are various and they have many aspects. If they are not pointed out, how can we know what direction to take? I will now explain them in general for the great assembly. There are eight aspects of a resolve: deviant, proper, true, false, great, small, partial, and complete.

What is meant by **deviant, proper, true, false, great, small, partial, and complete?** A cultivator's resolve is deviant if in his practice he does not investigate his own mind but knows only about external matters. Perhaps he seeks benefit and offerings, likes fame and a good reputation, is greedy for objects of pleasure in the present, or he may hope for reward in the future. A resolve such as this is deviant.

When a cultivator seeks neither gain nor fame and has no greed either for pleasure or for rewards, but wishes only to settle the matter of birth and death, and to attain Bodhi, then his resolve is proper.

Commentary:

But, since the situation is like this; we certainly must resolve upon Bodhi and make firm vows, or else we will never become Buddhas and never reach our goals. **Resolves and vows are various.** Peoples' wishes are of many different kinds. **And they have many aspects.** A resolve comes from a person's thinking, from his goals, his will, and his intent. There are many different aspects involved, 84000, you could say. **If they are not pointed out,** if I don't explain them in general to show them to you, **how can we know what direction to take?** How shall we know that we should stride forward in progress? How could we know the goal? **I will now explain them in general for the great assembly.** Great Master Sying An says, "Now, for the entire assembly, I will describe them in general." **There are eight aspects of a resolve:** in general, these eight describe the kind of resolve: **deviant, proper, true, false, great, small, partial, and complete.**

In explaining these eight, we can use the Six Guiding Principles of the City of Ten Thousand Buddhas to describe the kind of resolve we should have. To be deviant is to always be selfish. To be proper is to benefit others and gain no personal benefit. To be false is to do things for personal gain, not for the benefit of others. To have a small resolve means that you do things for personal gain. Such smallness will lead to fighting, seeking, and being greedy for personal profit; it involves having only oneself in view. If we can do things for everyone's good, be proper and unbiased, make universal offerings, take the Dharma Realm as our substance, and take empty space as our function, then that is great. To have a great resolve means that we wish to benefit others.

Partial refers to being biased and cleaving to a minority, a small part of the whole. Complete refers to comprising everything and excluding nothing. A verse well describes the aspect of being complete:

> With the Dharma Realm as our substance,
>   what is there outside?
> With all of empty space as our function,
>   everything is contained.
> The myriad things are all level and equal,
>   let discriminations go
> To where words have never traveled, and
> Before a single thought comes forth.

What could be outside the Dharma Realm? Empty space is the great function of people; it contains everything. See that everything that happens is all the same. This is to be complete.

These aspects are described in detail in the text that follows.

What is meant by deviant, proper, true, false, great, small, partial, and complete?

What is a deviant resolve?

A cultivator's resolve is deviant if in his practice he does not investigate his own mind but knows about only external matters.

"A cultivator" refers to a monastic. In this case, he practices, but merely puts on a good show. He might perform repentance ceremonies, bow to the Buddhas, and also recite sutras; he is putting on a show for people around him. He doesn't return the light and look within: "Am I repenting in my heart? Am I bowing in my heart to the Buddhas? Am I reciting sutras in my heart?" If he is reciting inside, then he is being true. But his resolve is deviant if he is simply putting on a show, pretending to be an old-hand at cultivating, and advertises whatever work he does. He, for example, waits until others are coming his way, then he starts sweeping the walkways, putting on a show. Since he is putting on a show, not only does he fail to generate merit and virtue, he becomes deviant and improper. He advertises his shows and tells others how he helps them, hoping they will appreciate him. We should be clear about this deviant aspect and understand this saying:

> We help others,
>> and seek nothing in return,
> We teach others,
>> but not so that they will owe us a favor.

We help others whenever we can, but shouldn't keep in mind a list of what we've done for others and broadcast the news, "Did you know? I renovated that temple!" He points out the dedication plaques bearing his name, fearing that others might not see what he has done. Thus he **seeks benefit and offerings**. Someone with a proper resolve would never behave like that; deviant and proper is a matched pair of opposites.

Deviance is *yin*. Properness is *yang*. Deviant people can't face up to the light of day. Proper people shine forth a bright light, they are full of light, and their behavior is correct in any given circumstance.

"In his practice he does not investigate his own mind." He doesn't work on his own nature; instead, he looks outside himself, and "knows about only external matters." He might perform repentance ceremonies for others, or recite sutras for others, putting on a big show and becoming exhausted everyday. And he tells everyone of his labors, pretending to be a great philanthropist, blabbing to everyone, letting the story out. He doesn't humbly mask his talents while correcting his own faults. Why does he advertise? He is looking for benefits; he wants others to make offerings to him and believe in him. He wants people to give him special gifts. Give a cultivator special gifts and you might cause him to stop cultivating; therefore, no one should give special gifts to others and make special offerings to one single person.

Or he **likes fame and a good reputation,** enjoys having others spread the word that he is an old-hand at cultivating the Way, a grand cultivator, and truly fine. Or like others who pretend to be monastics, but actually eat meat, drink alcohol, and play around, he is **greedy for objects of pleasure in the present.** Such people hanker for temporal pleasures. They might even have palatial temples and live like kings. Don't be fooled by any show they may put on; what does it matter that their temples are as fancy as imperial palaces? Even a king can fall to lower realms. They might **hope for reward in the future.** They think, "By doing these good deeds now, in future lives I'll be a king and have everything the way I want." **A resolve such as this is deviant.**

What is it like **when a cultivator seeks neither gain nor fame?** What does it mean to be proper? One **has no greed either for pleasure or for rewards,** or enjoying luxuries, or taking vacation trips to amusement parks. One **wishes only to settle the matters of birth and death,** to end birth and death, **and to attain Bodhi,** seeking true and proper wisdom. **Then his resolve is proper.** The resolve is deviant if a person doesn't wish to settle the matter of birth and death. Cultivators must be clear about this point, or else they can cultivate for a long time, but what they do will still be the karma of demons. They might cultivate a long time, but they still will be part of the demon king's retinue.

Essay:

If, in moment after moment, he seeks the path of the Buddhas above; in thought after thought, he transforms living beings below; if he hears that the road to Buddhahood is long and far, yet does not retreat in fear; if he observes that beings

are hard to transform, yet does not become weary; if he proceeds as though climbing a ten-thousand-foot mountain, determined to reach the summit or proceeds as though ascending a nine-storied stupa, fixed upon advancing to the top, then his resolve is true.

If he commits offenses but does not repent of them; if he has faults but does not change them; if he is turbid inside but makes a show of purity; if he is diligent at the start but lax later on; if he has good intentions but mixes them with a quest for name and gain; if he does wholesome practices, but defiles them with the karma created by committing offenses, then his resolve is false.

"When the realm of living beings has come to an end, then my vows will end. When the Bodhi Way is realized, then my vows will be fulfilled." Such a resolve is great. If he views the Triple Realm as a prison; if he treats birth and death as an enemy; if he intends to save only himself and has no wish to save others, then his resolve is small.

Commentary:

If, in moment after moment, he seeks the path of the Buddhas above, this aspect of a resolve describes someone who has his mind on what he is doing, and thinks of nothing else. What does he think of? "He seeks the path of the Buddhas above." The path that leads to Buddhahood. In thought after thought, he transforms living beings below. We must do good deeds if we want to become Buddhas. We can't expect to become a Buddha without expending even the slightest bit of effort. We must perform acts of merit and service. How? By teaching and transforming living beings, enabling them to give up any deviant or false ways they have and return to what is proper and true. If we can thus cause living beings to wake up, then we will be doing good deeds in Buddhism.

He hears that the road to Buddhahood is long and far, yet does not retreat in fear. Becoming a Buddha is not easy. The road to Buddhahood is long and far. It took Shakyamuni Buddha three major asamkhyeya kalpas to become a Buddha. Even one asamkhyeya kalpa is a measureless number; "asamkhyeya" is the Sanskrit for "a measureless number," and it took three major "measureless numbers." So someone may hear of this long time involved and heave an exasperated sigh of despair, or even become frightened, thinking, "How shall I ever cultivate for such a long time?" Like when we read the Buddhist sutras and think, "This sutra is so long; when shall I ever finish reading it? How will I ever learn to memorize the whole thing?" These are all examples of thoughts of retreat. Here, however, you don't think of retreating even though Buddhahood is a long way off. Instead, you are vigorous, never forgetting the basic duties of a cultivator of the Way.

He observes that beings are hard to transform, yet does not become weary. Teaching living beings is difficult indeed. Try to get them to stop their bad habits and instead of stopping, they will pursue those bad habits even more. Living beings are strange in this way. Try and help them, and they won't accept your help. They are hard to save, so we might become weary or fed up unless our resolve is proper.

If he proceeds as though climbing a ten-thousand-foot mountain, or a thirty-thousand foot mountain or even a thirty-thousand mile high mountain, the point being, a lofty mountain, **determined to reach the summit** of that mountain, **or proceeds as though ascending a nine-storied stupa,** a jeweled pagoda, **fixed upon advancing to the top, then his resolve is true.** A resolve like that, where we don't give up half-way or quit before we get there, but see it through to the end, indicates a proper resolve upon Bodhi. However, **if he commits offenses but does not repent of them,** then although he makes mistakes, he conceals them, is not frank, and does not confess to everyone and reform. **If he has faults but does not change them,** then although he plainly has a problem, he claims that his vices are ingrained habit patterns from time immemorial and is unable to change his ways. He is simply unwilling to get rid of his faults. **If he is turbid inside but makes a show of purity,** then in his heart he is jealous, obstructive, stupid, full of false thinking, arrogant, and full of doubt, but puts on a show to others of being pure and lofty. **If he is diligent at the start but lax later on,** then the vigor he showed when he first left home to cultivate flags. He never sees it through; his strength gives out. **If he** might have **good intentions but mixes them with a quest for name and gain**, then his motives in doing good deeds is to get a good reputation, so he tries to pull the wool over peoples' eyes and make a good name for himself. Everything he does is for name and gain; nothing he does is truly for the sake of the Buddhadharma. **If he does wholesome practices,** even though those methods are good, he **defiles them with the karma created by committing offenses,** doing very sordid, messy things, like some of the things that happen when those who claim to be Buddhists of the secret school cheat people, carry on, and get involved in scandalous deeds.

"This is the secret-school," they claim, "That's the way we do things in the secret-school." They are just mortally wounding other people. And ignorant followers blindly obey, believing that the secret-school is the most esoteric sect of Buddhism, and they get banned and dragged into the mess. If he has resolved upon Bodhi for these reasons **then his resolve is false**. He is a phony.

When the realm of living beings has come to an end. What is the great resolve? It is the wish to save all living beings. Earth Store Bodhisattva exhibits such resolve, for example, in his vow that:

> Only when the hells are empty
>> will I become a Buddha;
> Only when all living beings are saved
>> will I accomplish Bodhi.

And when all afflictions are gone, **then my vows will end.** When all living beings have been saved then my vow power will be finished. **When the Bodhi Way is realized,** when my cultivation of the road to enlightenment and to becoming a Buddha is completed, **then my vows will be fulfilled**; they will have been successful. **Such a resolve is great.** Nothing is greater than this. This is the resolve of a Bodhisattva.

If he views the Triple Realm, the desire realm, the form realm, and the formless realm, **as a prison**; **if he treats birth and death as an enemy**; then he has a viewpoint of the Theravada. The arhats see the world this way. They see the cycle of being born and dying over and over again as an enemy. **If he intends to save only himself and has no wish to save others, then his resolve is small.** "Small" means that one is narrow-minded. "Great" means that one is broad-minded.

Essay:

If he sees living beings as existing outside of his mind; if he does wish to save others and to realize Buddhahood, but does not forget his own accumulation of merit and does not get rid of his worldly knowledge and views, then his resolve is partial. If he knows that his own nature is the same as living beings and, therefore, vows to save them; if he knows that his own nature is the same as the Buddha Path and, therefore, vows to realize it; if he does not see even one thing as existing apart from the mind; if his mind is like empty space; if he makes vows that are like empty space; if he cultivates practices that are like empty space; if he attains a fruition like empty space, and yet does not grasp at the characteristic of empty space, then his resolve is complete.

Having understood these eight different aspects of a resolve, we should know how to investigate and contemplate them. Knowing how to investigate and contemplate them, we know which to keep and which to discard. Knowing which to keep and which to discard, we can then resolve our minds.

**What does it mean to "investigate and contemplate them?"
We must ask ourselves, "Which of these eight aspects does my
resolve have? Is my resolve deviant or proper, true or false,
great or small, partial or complete?" What does it mean to
"keep or discard?" It means that we discard the deviant, the
false, the small, and the partial, and that we keep the proper,
the true, the great, and the complete. To make a resolve in this
way is truly and properly to resolve upon Bodhi.**

Commentary:

**If he sees living beings as existing outside of his mind; if he
does wish to save others and to become a Buddha,** he does want
to save the other living beings he perceives to be outside his own
mind, and does want to perfect the path of becoming a Buddha
which he perceives to be outside of his own mind, **but does not
forget his own accumulation of merit.** He is always thinking of
the merits of saving living beings and becoming a Buddha. He
becomes very attached to the idea **and does not get rid of his
worldly knowledge and views.** Not being able to wipe out his
deviant knowledge and deviant views, **his resolve is partial.** If he
is always attached to these things inside, his resolve is false. He
doesn't understand the complete doctrine. He still has bias, partial
views.

If he knows that his own nature is the same as living beings
then he knows that living beings are not apart from his own nature.
Living beings are inside of his own nature. He **therefore, vows to
save them.** He vows to save the living beings of his own nature,
vows to sever the afflictions of his own nature, vows to study the
Dharma doors of his own nature, and vows to accomplish the path
of his own nature that leads to becoming a Buddha.

**If he knows that his own nature is the same as the Buddha
Path and,** he wants to accomplish the Buddha Path of his own
nature, then he **vows to realize it.** He wants to become a Buddha
because Buddhahood is not apart from his own nature. **If he does
not see even one thing as existing apart from the mind,** then

there is nothing to become attached to, and no one should have any attachment to anything. If one thinks that there are things outside of one's own nature that can be studied, and one seeks the Dharma outside of one's own nature, then such people have entered an externalist path.

How should one be? **If his mind is like empty space; if he makes vows that are** vast **like empty space; if he cultivates practices that are like empty space,** and everything he does is like empty space, **if he attains a fruition** as big as **empty space, and yet does not grasp at the characteristic of empty space,** then he is not attached to thinking that empty space has any certain characteristic. An attachment would take place were he to ascribe any certain characteristic to empty space. If he makes a resolve in this way, **then his resolve is complete**.

Having understood these eight different aspects of a resolve, and their characteristics, **we know how to investigate and contemplate them** in detail. **Knowing how to investigate and contemplate them, we know which to keep,** which aspects we want, **and which to discard,** and which aspects we don't want. **Knowing which to keep and which to discard, we can then resolve our minds.**

What does it mean to "investigate and contemplate them?" How do we find out? **We must ask ourselves, "Which of these eight aspects does my resolve have? Is my resolve deviant or proper, true or false, great or small, partial or complete?"** We should ask ourselves. **What does it mean to "keep or discard?"** After asking ourselves and recognizing our own resolve, **it means that we discard** and get rid of **the deviant, the false, the small, and the partial, and that we keep the proper, the true, the great, and the complete. To make a resolve in this way is truly and properly to resolve upon Bodhi.** If we understand how to resolve upon Bodhi as described above, in the future, we can perfect a Bodhi like empty space.

Ten Causes and Conditions

Essay:

The resolve upon Bodhi is the foremost among all good things. It can arise only due to certain causes and conditions. In general, there are ten causes and conditions, which will now be discussed. What are the ten?

The first is mindfulness of the Buddhas' deep kindness.

The second is mindfulness of our parents' kindness.

The third is mindfulness of our teachers' and elders' kindness.

The fourth is mindfulness of donors' kindness.

The fifth is mindfulness of living beings' kindness.

The sixth is mindfulness of the suffering in birth and death.

The seventh is reverence for our own spiritual nature.

The eighth is repenting of karmic obstacles and reforming.

The ninth is the wish for rebirth in the Pure Land.

The tenth is the wish to cause the Proper Dharma to remain in the world for a long time.

Commentary:

The resolve upon Bodhi is the resolve to seek wisdom, to seek enlightenment to the Path, which is the opposite of confusion. We living beings are unenlightened about the Way, and, therefore, are unable to resolve upon Bodhi. Once we understand about the Way, we can resolve upon Bodhi. This resolve **is the foremost among all good things**. No good deed you could do is as important as this resolve on Bodhi. **It can arise only due to certain causes and conditions.** There certainly must have been causes planted and conditions that aid your resolve upon Bodhi. Causes are the main reasons; conditions are the supporting factors for development. Why would you want to resolve upon Bodhi? **In general, there are ten causes and conditions, which will now be discussed. What are the ten? The first is mindfulness of the Buddhas' deep kindness.** We living beings are unaware of how kind the Buddha is to us. He is kind, compassionate, joyful, and impartial. There is no way to describe the Buddha's kindness. It could never be completely spoken of. The Buddha, for three asamkhyeya kalpas, cultivated blessings and wisdom, and, for a hundred kalpas, planted the seeds of the Buddhas' perfect appearance. For the single goal of saving you, me, and all living beings, the goal that we stop suffering and find happiness, the Buddha personally endured all kinds of unbearable hardships while cultivating to reach the position for which he can help us. Thus, the Buddha's kindness is the most significant.

The second is mindfulness of our parents' kindness. Our parents' kindness, from carrying us, bearing us, feeding us, and raising us, is another debt we will find hard to repay.

The third is mindfulness of our teachers' and elders' kindness. "Teachers" refers to those who teach us Dharma and other ways of wisdom. We should also repay the debt we owe them for their toil in employing many clever ways to teach us.

The fourth is mindfulness of donors' kindness. We have left the home life to cultivate the Path. "Donors" are our Dharma-protectors; they support us as we cultivate the Way. And so this kindness is another debt we must repay. If we fail to make the resolve upon Bodhi, it will be a debt that is hard to repay. As it is said, "If you haven't put an end to the three minds, then even a cup of water is hard to digest." Even a cup of water a donor gives you will be hard to digest if you haven't stopped the three minds and haven't resolved upon Bodhi.

The fifth is mindfulness of living beings' kindness. All living beings, too, have been kind to us. We have had ties with them all, and so should repay their kindness.

The sixth reason for resolving on Bodhi **is mindfulness of the** pain and **suffering** involved in being **in birth and death.**

The seventh is reverence for our own spiritual nature. All we living beings have the Buddha nature and can become Buddhas. We should, therefore, resolve to reach Bodhi and fully realize our potential to become Buddhas. We must revere our inherent, spiritual, enlightened nature.

The eighth reason for resolving upon Bodhi **is repenting of karmic obstacles and reforming,** eradicating your karmic offenses.

The ninth is the wish for rebirth in the Pure Land, the Western Land of Ultimate Bliss, and to see Amitabha Buddha.

The tenth is the wish to cause the Proper Dharma to remain in the world for a long time. We resolve upon Bodhi and cultivate the Way. The Proper Dharma Age will exist in this world only when there are people truly cultivating the Way. It will not exist in this world if no one truly cultivates the Way.

In light of these ten reasons, we should all resolve upon Bodhi. Quickly resolve to reach Bodhi! Don't think that it doesn't affect other people if we cultivate or not. All beings in this world have an effect on each other. The Buddhadharma will remain in this world for a long time if we resolve upon Bodhi. The Buddhadharma will die out if any of us fail to resolve on Bodhi.

The Buddha's Deep Kindness

Essay:

What is mindfulness of the Buddha's deep kindness? After our Thus Come One Shakyamuni first made his resolve, he walked the Bodhisattva Path for our sakes and passed through an infinite number of kalpas, enduring all manner of suffering. When I create bad karma, the Buddha pities me and with expedient means teaches and transforms me. I, however, remain ignorant and do not know how to accept the teaching with faith. When I fall into the hells, the Buddha again compassionately feels the pain and wishes to undergo suffering on my behalf. But my karma is heavy, and I cannot be pulled out. When I am reborn as a human, the Buddha uses expedient means to cause me to plant roots of goodness. In life after life, he follows me and does not forsake me in his thoughts for an instant.

When the Buddha first appeared in the world, I was still sunk in the lower realms. Now that I have a human body, the Buddha has already passed into still quietude. What are my offenses that have caused me to be born in the Dharma Ending Age? What are my blessings that have made it possible for me to leave the home and family life? What are my obstacles that have prevented me from seeing his golden body? What good fortune has made it possible for me to encounter his sharira? I contemplate in that way. **If I did not plant good roots in the past, how else could I be able to hear the Buddhadharma? And if I had never heard the Buddhadharma, how could I know that the Buddha is always kind to me?**

His kindness and his virtue are greater than the highest mountain. **If I fail to make a vast and great resolve to cultivate the Bodhisattva Path and to establish the Buddhadharma in order to save living beings, even to the point that in making this effort my bones wear away and my body is wrecked, then how can I possibly hope to repay his kindness? This is the first cause and condition for making the resolve to attain Bodhi.**

Commentary:

What is mindfulness of the Buddha's deep kindness? This is the first cause and condition.

After our founding teacher **Thus Come One Shakyamuni first made his resolve** – why did the Buddha resolve his mind on Bodhi? **He walked the Bodhisattva Path for our sakes.** For the single wish to save us living beings, the Buddha resolved to attain Bodhi and practiced the Bodhisattva Path, which lead him to benefit others in life after life.

The Buddha **passed through an infinite number of** great **kalpas, enduring all manners of suffering. When I create bad karma, the Buddha pities me.** When we create bad karma, the Buddha pities us and wishes to take the suffering for us. **And with** various clever **expedient means** and analogies to explain and clarify things, he **teaches and transforms me,** helping me to mend my evil ways, turn over a new leaf to become a good person, and to resolve upon Bodhi.

I, however, remain ignorant and do not know how to accept the teaching with faith. The Buddha is so kind and compassionate to us, but we are dull and aren't even aware of the Buddha's kindness, and don't know enough to accept the Buddha's teaching. **When I fall into the hells, the Buddha again compassionately**

feels the pain. When the Buddha sees a living being fall into the hells, it is as if he himself were falling in – it is equally unbearable. The Buddha **wishes to undergo suffering on my behalf. But my karma is heavy, and I cannot be pulled out.** Our karmic obstacles are too heavy, and we can't be saved.

But after the Buddha devises the right methods to save us from the hells, **when I am reborn as a human, the Buddha uses** many kinds of clever and **expedient means** and Dharma doors **to cause me to plant good roots. In life after life, he follows me.** The *Avatamsaka Sutra* relates how the Bodhisattva accompanies living beings into the hells, becomes an animal with the living beings, and becomes a hungry ghost when the living beings do, in order to be with the beings and be able to influence them to resolve upon Bodhi and cultivate. When the beings become human again, so does the Bodhisattva, always accompanying living beings as they go through their sufferings. The Buddha **does not forsake me in his thoughts for an instant,** not for even a split-second.

When the Buddha Shakyamuni **first appeared in the world, I was still sunk in the lower realms** – in the hells, among the animals, or one of the hungry ghosts. **Now that I have a human body, the Buddha has already passed into still quietude.** Through the Buddha's help I have been able to become a human being again, but the Buddha has already entered Nirvana. **What are my offenses that have caused me to be born in the Dharma Ending Age?** We obviously have grave karmic offenses that have caused us to be born in the Dharma Ending Age; if not, we would be born at a time when we could see the Buddha and hear him speak Dharma. **What are my blessings that have made it possible for me to leave the home and family life?** This essay was written with monastics in mind. Although we have offenses, we also have blessings that have enabled us to leave the home-life. **What are my** karmic **obstacles that have prevented me from seeing** the Buddha's **golden body? What good fortune has made it possible for me to encounter his sharira?** In the Dharma Ending Age, I'm lucky enough to be able to see the Buddha's sharira. **I contemplate**

in that way. I think things over in light of the previously mentioned facts.

If I did not plant good roots in the past, if I hadn't ever planted any good roots in the past, **how else could I be able to hear the Buddhadharma?** You won't be able to hear the Buddhadharma unless in the past you have planted good roots. **And if I had never heard the Buddhadharma, how could I know that the Buddha is always kind to me?** I wouldn't know how kind the Buddha is to me unless I have heard the Buddhadharma.

His kindness and his virtue are greater than the highest mountain, and deeper than any ocean. The Buddha is so kind to us, **if I fail to make a vast and great resolve to cultivate the Bodhisattva Path and to establish the Buddhadharma,** with any strength I have, **in order to save living beings, even to the point that in making this effort my bones wear away and my body is wrecked,** if we fail to do our utmost to set up and propagate the Buddhas' teachings, **then how can I possibly hope to repay his kindness?** We'll never finish repaying the Buddha's kindness.

This is the first cause and condition for making the resolve to attain Bodhi. This is the first of the ten causes and conditions; we think of the Buddha's kindness and thus resolve upon Bodhi.

Our Parents' Kindness

Essay:

What is mindfulness of our parents' kindness? Alas for my parents! I was born through much toil. I was nurtured nine months in the womb and was suckled three years at the breast. My bottom was dried and my diapers were changed. I was fed delicacies while my parents toiled bitterly. Only then was I able to grow up. They hoped only that I might glorify and carry on the family name and continue the ritual offerings to our ancestors. But now I have left the home and family, and am gratuitously called a disciple of Shakyamuni and have dared to assume the title of Shramana. I neither offer delicacies to my parents nor sweep the ancestral graves. While they live, I cannot take care of their physical needs; after they depart, I cannot guide their souls. In this world, I have thereby hurt them greatly, and as they leave this world, I am of no real help. To cause them such a double loss is a serious offense. How can I possibly avoid the consequences!

I contemplate in this way: I must always cultivate the Buddhas' Path through hundreds of kalpas and in thousands of lives and save living beings everywhere throughout the ten directions and three periods of time. I will rescue not only my parents of this life but will do the same for my parents of every life. **I will save not only one person's parents but everyone's parents.**

This is the second cause and condition for making the resolve to attain Bodhi.

Commentary:

What is mindfulness of our parents' kindness? Alas for my parents! "Alas!" expresses the deep feeling for them that we should always have. **I was born through much toil.** These two opening lines are similar to lines in the Book of Odes, a Chinese classic. **I was nurtured nine months in the womb and was suckled three years at the breast. My bottom was dried and my diapers were changed,** meaning, while an infant, I was cared for by my mother. She kept me dry and clean. **I was fed delicacies while my parents toiled bitterly.** My mother took all the bitter pills, and gave me all the sweets. **Only then was I able to grow up.** Only through such parental care is the child able to grow and mature.

They hoped only that I might glorify and carry on the family name. Their only wish for me is that I continue their line and carry on the good family reputation. **And continue the ritual offerings to our ancestors.** The custom of offspring to honor and make ritual offerings to past relatives and ancestors. **But now I have left the home and family,** I'm already a monk, **and am gratuitously called a disciple of Shakyamuni.** Here Master Sying An means that he is called a disciple of Shakyamuni Buddha, whether or not he meets the requirements. I have **dared to assume the title of Shramana.** Again, the master speaks humbly, saying that he shamelessly dares to assume the title of Shramana, but feels that he does not meet the requirements; he says he is just pretending, just a filler who makes up the numbers, but can't actually fill the position. "Shramana" is one who "diligently cultivates precepts, samadhi, and wisdom, and stops greed, hatred, and stupidity."

I neither offer delicacies to my parents nor sweep the ancestral graves. Master Sying An, as a monk, no longer personally serves his parents nor performs the ritual sweeping of the grave site and ritual offerings. **While they live, I cannot take care of their physical needs**. Left-home people don't support their parents in material ways. **After they depart, I cannot guide their souls.** Even as monastics we may not be advanced enough to be able to guide our parents' departed souls to a blissful resting place.

In this world, I have thereby hurt them greatly, from a worldly, social viewpoint, **and as they leave this world, I am of no real help.** I have had no success in my cultivation of world-transcending methods of practice and am unable to help them through my progress in cultivation. **To cause them such a double loss is a serious offense.** As they live, I don't support them; when they pass away, I don't make ritual remembrances. I've left the secular lifestyle and don't meddle in my secular family's business. But I've "caused them such a double loss," **how can I possibly avoid the consequences!**

I contemplate in this way: I must always cultivate the Buddhas' Path through hundreds of kalpas and in thousands of lives. What should I do? I must always cultivate the Buddhas' Path, continuing to practice constantly. **And** I must **save living beings everywhere throughout the ten directions and three periods of time,** the past, present, and future, in order to repay the kindness of my parents. **I will rescue not only my parents of this life but will do the same for my parents of every life. I will save not only one person's parents but everyone's parents,** enabling them to be reborn in the heavens.

> When one child attains the Path,
> Nine generations are reborn in the heavens.

If we do a good job of cultivating, then we can cause those people related to us through nine generations past, and even everyone's parents to ascend. **This is the second cause and condition for making the resolve to attain Bodhi.**

Our Teachers' and Elders' Kindness

Essay:

What is mindfulness of our teachers' and elders' kindness? My parents bore me and raised me, but if not for educators and elders, I would know nothing of propriety or righteousness. If not for spiritual teachers and elders, I would understand nothing of the Buddhadharma. One who knows nothing of propriety or righteousness may be considered a mere animal. One who understands nothing of the Buddhadharma is no different than an ordinary person. Now we know the rudiments of propriety and righteousness and have a rough understanding of the Buddhadharma.

The kashaya sash covers our bodies; the various precepts permeate our being. We have obtained these through the deep kindness of our teachers and elders. If we seek a small accomplishment, we can benefit only ourselves. Within the Great Vehicle our wish is to benefit all people. In that way, we can benefit both secular and world-transcending teachers and elders.

This is the third cause and condition for making the resolve to attain Bodhi.

Commentary:

What is mindfulness of my teachers' and elders' kindness? Why do we say that we should be mindful of repaying the kindness of our teachers and elders? Repaying the kindness of our parents was previously discussed; they gave birth to our physical bodies, and so we are deeply indebted to them. Now we are going to learn of the kindness of our teachers and elders. Teachers are models of holding the rules. Under them, one studies the rules and regulations. A teacher is lofty and surpasses the common lot.

My parents bore me and raised me, but if not for educators and elders, I would know nothing of propriety or righteousness. They teach and transform by imparting knowledge to me. "Propriety" refers to behaviour that shows courtesy and of respect. "Righteousness" means possessing integrity, patriotism, and a public spirit. General Guan Gong of the Three Kingdoms period was known for his "magnificent, righteous loyalty that was loftier than the skies." He was dedicated to protecting his emperor, Liu Bei. He could not be bribed or made a tool of by others. Although General Cao Cao tried to trick him into deserting, Guan Gong never compromised his principles.

If you greet people by respectfully making a half-bow, and showing them deference, they will certainly not scold you in return. People might scold if you are rude and impolite to them. People might scold you anyway – some people even scold monks like me. But I don't get angry and say, "You've scolded me; well then, I'll make you fall into the Avici (Relentless) hells!" Instead think, "I'll take them across to Buddhahood. If they don't reach Buddhahood, I won't either."

Propriety and righteousness must be understood by people in the world. We must not fail to understand propriety and know of righteousness. We must never neglect to do righteous deeds; we must do things properly, exactly, and correctly! In this way, each of us can be righteous. We can also be righteous by helping others, even if doing so means taking a personal loss. Let us forego selfishness and help others instead.

Educators instruct their students in all aspects of propriety. They teach us to be polite and to avoid scolding others. We differ from animals because of our propriety. The behaviour of people who fail to respect others may be considered mere animals. But even animals respond cordially to one another! How can we humans fail to be polite? Propriety is one of the Eight Virtues:

1. Filial gratitude
2. Fraternal respect
3. Loyalty
4. Trustworthiness
5. Propriety
6. Righteousness
7. Virtue
8. Sense of shame

We should be respectful and have a righteous regard for others. Were it not for the education offered by our teachers, we would not understand how to behave as people.

If not for spiritual teachers and elders, I would understand nothing of the Buddhadharma. Those who wish to cultivate the Path definitely must find a Bright-eyed Good and Wise Advisor. What are the requisites of a Good and Wise Advisor? First, he must not be greedy for wealth. Second, he must not be greedy for material objects nor be lustful. Third, he must not seek fame. Fourth, he must not be selfish. Use this checklist; does he direct others to do things so that he will gain the advantage? Does he always plot to widen the scope of his own name and fame, and to promote his position? A real Bright-eyed Good and Wise Advisor would never do anything to benefit himself or to get name and fame; instead, everything that he does is to help and benefit others. Those who do not find a Bright-eyed Good and Wise Advisor will not understand the Buddhadharma. Lacking that understanding, how will they transcend this world? Most essential to cultivating the Path is to take a personal loss and benefit others, something that worldly people do not wish to do.

One who knows nothing of propriety or righteousness may be considered a mere animal. Most animals do not understand propriety. There are some, however, like the crow that returns to care for its parents, and like the goat-kid that kneels respectfully to drink the mother goat's milk. These animals are filial. So the meaning here is that a person who does not understand propriety is like an unfilial animal. **One who understands nothing of the Buddhadharma is no different than an ordinary person.** If we cultivate but do not understand the Buddhadharma, then how do we differ from ordinary worldly people? We don't.

Now we know the rudiments of propriety and righteousness. "We," says Great Master Sying An, refers to all monks and nuns and all lay Buddhists. To "know the rudiments" is to get the general idea in very plain and simple terms, to get the gist of propriety, **and to have a rough understanding,** a small part, **of the Buddhadharma.**

The kashaya sash covers our bodies. The "kashaya," the precept sash, is worn by monks and nuns. So it says,

> One now receives the kashaya sash as a result of
> seeds for Bodhi that one planted in the past.

To leave home and enter monastic life is not an easy matter. Without good roots, you cannot do it at all or if you are able to do it, you will soon retreat. We should vow to enter the Path as a virgin youth in life after life. We want to make just that firm a resolve for Bodhi. Cultivation is very easy for those who have entered the Path as a virgin youth. On the other hand, cultivation is very hard for those who are not virgin youths. Of course they, too, can cultivate, but only with difficulty. The various precepts permeate our being. "The various precepts" are the five, the eight, the ten major and forty-eight minor Bodhisattva precepts, the two hundred and fifty Bhikshu precepts, and the three hundred and forty-eight Bhikshuni precepts. By taking and upholding these precepts, we obtain great benefits. A saying goes,

> When living beings receive the Buddhas' precepts,
> they immediately enter the Buddhas' position.
>
> Brahma Net Sutra

One receives the Vajra Light Jeweled Precept Substance. **We have obtained these through the deep kindness of our teachers and elders.** Because of their intense kindness, we obtain the kashaya sash and the various precepts. And after we have obtained such rare treasures, **if we seek a small accomplishment, we can benefit only ourselves.** If we do not cultivate the Great Vehicle practices, but cultivate only the methods of the lesser vehicle, then we can only become enlightened to the fruition of arhatship. Attaining arhatship is good. However, it benefits only oneself not others, enlightens oneself not others, and saves oneself not others.

Within the Great Vehicle our wish is to benefit all people. In that way, we can benefit both secular and world-transcending teachers and elders.

This is the third cause and condition for making the resolve to attain Bodhi.

The Donors' Kindness

Essay:

What is mindfulness of donors' kindness? None of the materials we use in our daily lives belongs to us. Porridge and rice for our two meals, clothing for the four seasons, medicines for our illnesses – all the expenses for our physical needs – come through the strength of others. In order to provide for us, they work hard to plow the fields, yet can barely provide for themselves, while we sit comfortably to receive our food and still feel dissatisfied. Our donors spin and weave without cease and still suffer hardship, while we are comfortable, with more clothes than we can wear. We are even unaware that we should cherish what we have.

They live to the ends of their days in poor and humble dwellings amid nerve-wracking clamor, while we dwell among vast courtyards and in vacant halls amid refinement and ease throughout the year. They offer the fruits of their labors to supply our idleness; how can our hearts be at peace? Is it reasonable to use others' goods to nourish our own bodies? If we fail to be both compassionate and wise and to adorn ourselves with both blessings and wisdom, so that the faithful donors are blessed with kindness and living beings receive bounty, then even one grain of rice or one inch of thread will incur a debt. It will be hard to escape an evil retribution.

This is the fourth cause and condition for making the resolve to attain Bodhi.

Commentary:

What is mindfulness, not repaying, but not forgetting donors' kindness? None of the materials we use in our daily lives belongs to us. The essentials we use everyday aren't ours; others offer them to us. Morning porridge and rice at lunch for our two meals, clothing for the four seasons, all the clothes we wear, medicines for our illnesses – all the expenses for our physical needs, what we wear and eat – come through the strength of others. Others offer them to us to support us while we cultivate the Path.

In order to provide for us, they work hard to plow the fields, farmers sweat and toil, yet can barely provide for themselves, sometimes they are even without food. While we sit comfortably to receive our food and still feel dissatisfied. We do no work, but still have food, and get picky, finding this dish tastes bad and that dish is no good. Our donors spin and weave without cease and still suffer hardship, it requires much hard work to weave a piece of cloth. Yet we are comfortable, with more clothes than we can wear. We are even unaware that we should cherish and take care of what we have.

They live to the ends of their days in poor broken-down and humble dwellings amid nerve-wracking clamor, never getting even a moments peace, while we dwell among vast courtyards and in vacant halls amid refinement and ease throughout the year. We live comfortably and free in large buildings with well maintained yards.

They offer the fruits of their labors to supply our idleness; how can our hearts be at peace? We supply our own idleness through others' work; how can we feel good about this in our hearts? Is it reasonable to use others goods to nourish our own bodies? No, it is not reasonable. What should we do?

If we fail to be both compassionate and wise, cultivating the contemplation of compassion and the contemplation of wisdom, **and to adorn ourselves with both blessings and wisdom,** cultivating blessings and wisdom, then transferring that **so the faithful donors are blessed with kindness and living beings receive bounty, then even one grain of rice or one inch of thread will incur a debt,** to be repaid in the future.

> One grain of rice offered by a faithful donor
> Is as heavy as Mount Sumeru.
> If we eat it and fail to cultivate the Path,
> We'll toil as beasts of burden to repay it.

Those of old also said,

> "Even water is hard to digest if you fail to stop thoughts about past, present and future."

If someone makes an offering of a glass of water, it will be hard to digest if we drink it but fail to cultivate. **It will be hard to escape an evil retribution,** and the debts will be repaid.

This is the fourth cause and condition for making the resolve to attain Bodhi.

Living Beings' Kindness

Essay:

What is mindfulness of living beings' kindness? In life after life, from distant kalpas onwards, every living being and I have been each other's father and mother. We have been kind to one another. Now although the passage of time has separated us, and in our confusion we do not recognize each other, it is only logical that we repay them for their toil. How do we know that we were not sons in lives past of those who are now fur-bearing and capped with horns? How do we know that those who now crawl on the ground and fly in the air were not our fathers in lives past?

Our parents constantly looked after us, but we left them when we were young; we have grown up and have forgotten their faces. Even less do we remember our family and friends of lives past, and now it is difficult to remember if we were once named Smith or Jones. As our ancestors wail and cry out in the hells, or are born over and over again as hungry ghosts, who can know of their suffering and pain? They are starving; to whom can they appeal? I cannot see or hear them, but they must be seeking rescue and release. The sutras reveal this situation with exceptional clarity. Only the Buddhas could have spoken these words. How could people with deviant views know of this?

For these reasons, Bodhisattvas observe that even grubs and ants were their parents in lives past and have the potential to be Buddhas in the future. They always think of benefiting them and remember to return their kindness.

This is the fifth cause and condition for making the resolve to attain Bodhi.

Commentary:

What is mindfulness of living beings' kindness? What does it mean to not forget the kindness shown us by all living beings? "Living beings" means all creatures, and there are twenty four kinds: those flying, walking, crawling, and rooted, those born from wombs, from eggs, from moisture, and from metamorphosis, those with or without form, those with or without appearance, and so forth. Even mosquitoes and ants are included here.

In life after life, from distant kalpas onwards, every living being and I have been each other's father and mother. They were my parents, I was theirs. They were my sons, I was theirs. We have been kind to one another. Now although the passage of time has separated us, although time has gone by, and in our confusion we do not recognize each other, it is only logical that we repay them for their toil. How do we know that we were not sons in lives past of those who are now fur-bearing and capped with horns? How do we know that we were not their sons or daughters in past lives? How do we know that those who now are very small and crawl on the ground and those tiny insects and bugs that fly in the air were not our fathers in lives past? Our parents constantly looked after us, but we left them when we were young; we have grown up and have forgotten their faces. We left them when we were young and now have even forgotten what they look like. Even less do we remember our family and friends, parents and children of lives past, and now it is difficult to remember if we were once named Smith or Jones. We can't remember.

As our ancestors wail and cry out in the hells, or are born over and over again as hungry ghosts, without being able to become free. **Who can know of their suffering and pain?** Yet who knows they are in pain? **They are starving; to whom can they appeal?** Who could they tell of their hunger? **I cannot see or hear them, but they must be seeking rescue and release.** They certainly must be looking for someone to save them.

The sutras reveal this situation with exceptional clarity. Nowhere else but in the sutras is all this explained so clearly. **Only the Buddhas could have spoken these words.** Only someone with the intelligence and wisdom of a Buddha could explain the detailed principle of past causes and their future retributions. **How could people with deviant views know of this?** They, of course, don't know about any of this. They don't even believe in cause and effect.

For these reasons, Bodhisattvas observe that even grubs and ants were their parents in lives past and have the potential to be Buddhas in the future. They always think of benefiting them and remember to return their kindness, and to repay their past parents' kindness. **This is the fifth cause and condition for making the resolve to attain Bodhi.**

Essay:

What is mindfulness of the suffering of birth and death? From distant kalpas onwards, living beings and I have always been involved in birth and death and have not attained liberation. Whether we have been among people or in the heavens, in this world or in another, we have risen and fallen uncountable times. We ascend or fall in an instant – suddenly a god, suddenly a human, suddenly an animal, a hungry ghost, or a denizen of the hells.

We leave the black gate at dawn but return at night. We climb out of the pit of iron briefly but then fall back in again. As we ascend the mountain of knives, our bodies are slashed until not a bit of flesh remains. As we climb the tree of swords, our

hearts are slit open. The hot iron does not cure hunger; swallowing it roasts the liver and intestines. The broth of boiling copper does not quench thirst; drinking it dissolves the flesh and bones. Sharp saws dismember the body; once cut, it comes back together again. Clever breezes fan the body; it dies but quickly returns to life. In the city of raging fire, we endure the sounds of bloodcurdling screams and wails. In the pot of boiling oil, we hear only cries of excruciating pain. The body begins to freeze and harden and resembles a blue lotus forming a bud. Then the flesh and veins crack open and the body looks like a red lotus in bloom.

In a single night, the denizens of the hells pass through ten thousand births and deaths. In a single morning, the sufferings in the hells are what humans would go through in a hundred years. The harried wardens of the hells become weary. Who believes that King Yama is not teaching us with this warning? Yet only while actually experiencing suffering do we know its bitterness, but our regrets come too late. Once free, we forget again, and then we create the same karma as before. We whip the mule until it bleeds; who could know that it is our mother in anguish? We lead the pig to slaughter; who could know that it is our father in agony? We eat our own sons without being aware, just like King Wen. And we gulp down our own relatives without recognizing them. This is the way of all ordinary people.

The loved ones of yesteryear are now sworn enemies. Rivals of days past are now our blood relatives. Our mothers of past lives are our wives of the present. Our fathers-in-law of old are now our husbands. Those with knowledge of past lives recognize these changes; they feel shame and embarrassment. Those with the Heavenly Eye see these situations; they find them ridiculous and pathetic.

Amid excrement and filth we pass nine difficult months. We emerge from the path of pus and blood in a pitiable state. When

young, we know nothing and cannot tell east from west. As
adults, we become more aware, but our greed and desire arises.
In an instant, old age and illness overtake us; suddenly death
arrives. Amid the blaze of wind and fire, our spirit becomes
disordered; our vital energies and blood are exhausted. Our
flesh and skin wither and dry up. We feel as if iron needles are
piercing our every pore and as if knives are hacking our every
orifice.

When the spirit leaves the body at death, it feels more pain
than does a live turtle having its shell ripped off before it is
thrown in the pot.

Commentary:

What is mindfulness of the suffering of birth and death?
What do the sufferings of birth and death entail? They include the
pain of being sick and of growing old and of myriad other
unpleasant circumstances.

At birth, the baby undergoes intense suffering and feels as if
two mountains were crushing him on either side. At death, the four
elements (earth, water, fire, and air) separate. It is not easy to leave
this stinking skin bag; that leaving is excruciatingly painful. Some
people say that at birth, the baby undergoes pain like that which a
live tortoise would experience if its shell were ripped off. At death,
you experience as much pain as would a live cow whose hide is torn
off.

From distant kalpas onwards, for kalpas beyond reckoning
until the present, **living beings and I have always been involved
in birth and death** in the sea of suffering and **have not attained
liberation.** We want to be liberated, so we cultivate today, yet
tomorrow we fool around, the next day we take it easy, the day after
that we think of eating a big feast, and we want to have a good drink
the following day. Thus, we lose our mindfulness and constantly
indulge in deviant thoughts. Without the resolve for the Way, we
cannot attain liberation.

We may be born, **whether we have been among people or in the heavens,** but when our heavenly blessings run out, we may fall into the hells. We spin around in the cycle of birth and death, unable to get out. **In this world or in another** – we may return to this planet or go to another – **we have risen and fallen uncountable times.** Perhaps we were originally Chinese, but we became American; or perhaps we were Americans, but we became Chinese. **We ascend or fall in an instant – suddenly a god, suddenly a human, suddenly an animal, a hungry ghost, or a denizen of the hells.** We may suddenly find ourselves in any one of these painful situations.

We leave the black gate, the gate to the hells, **at dawn but return at night.** We return to the hells immediately after leaving them. **We climb out of the pit of iron briefly, but then fall back in again.** We leave the hells, the pit full of implements of punishment such as iron axes, iron knives, iron beds, the mountain of knives, and the tree of swords. We return to this place of suffering after having just left it. **As we ascend the mountain of knives, our bodies are slashed until not a bit of flesh remains.** The blades on the mountain of knives slash open every bit of flesh on our bodies. **As we climb the tree of swords, our hearts are slit open.** Our skin is all slit open, as if we had a heart attack. **The hot iron does not cure hunger.** We eat hot iron pellets because we are famished and nothing else available, but **swallowing it roasts the liver and intestines.**

The broth of boiling copper does not quench thirst. When we take a drink, the liquid is not like water – it is molten copper. We drink it, but it does not quench our thirst. **Drinking it dissolves the flesh and bones**, melting them into nothing.

Sharp saws dismember the body. Razor-sharp saws cut the body apart. **Once cut, it comes back together again.** Once you are sliced into pieces, the winds of your karma, the **clever breezes fan the body; it dies but quickly returns to life.** Once you are dead, the clever breezes fan you back to life. When you come back to life, don't think you will buy a car or live in a beautiful house. Instead of enjoying a life of luxury, you have to undergo suffering. The sufferings are so unbearable that you wish you were dead, but you have to live to undergo your evil retribution.

In the city of raging fire, we endure the sounds of bloodcurdling screams and wails. In the blazing city of hells, the pain is cruel and unbearable, and the screams are pitiful. We are tossed **in the pot of boiling oil; we hear only cries of excruciating pain. The body begins to freeze and harden and resembles a blue lotus forming a bud.** The body is blue with cold and looks like the bud of a blue lotus flower. **Then the flesh and veins crack open and the body looks like a red lotus in bloom**. This describes the body as looking very pretty, like a red lotus in bloom.

In a single night, the denizens of the hells pass through ten thousand births and deaths. They undergo birth and death, death and birth, tens of thousands of times. **In a single morning, the sufferings in the hells are what the humans would go through in a hundred years.** When you are in excruciating pain, you feel that the time is either very long or very short. One day in the Heaven of the Four Heavenly Kings is five hundred years in the human realm. One day in the human realm is one hundred years in the hells. The sufferings that hell-beings undergo in one night are equivalent to what we would undergo during a hundred years.

The harried wardens of the hells become weary. The jailers are always tired because they have so many offenders to deal with. **Who believes that King Yama is not teaching us with this warning?** The painful states of the hells teach living beings to stop doing evil, but no one knows that King Yama is teaching us this.

Yet only while actually experiencing suffering do we know its bitterness, but our regrets come too late. Once free, we forget again. When we aren't suffering, we forget about our pain and about our regrets, **and then we commit the same karma as before.** We do the same deeds all over again. Once the wound heals, we forget our pain. During the time of suffering, we do all good deeds and avoid all evils. Once the pain is over, we start to kill, steal, engage in sexual misconduct and all sorts of evil deeds, and entertain improper false thoughts. Human beings are creatures without aim or genuine wisdom.

We whip the mule until it bleeds; who could know that it is our mother in anguish? Meat eaters don't understand the principle involved in past causes and future retributions. They don't realize that the mule they beat may have been a relative of theirs in the past. Not only mules, but ants, mosquitoes, bugs – any living, breathing creature – and I have been family members together. Many unclear causes remain. Ignorant of all this, people who scold and hit other beings are actually harming their own flesh and blood. As the Buddha said,

> "All men have been my father;
> All women have been my mother."

And we might also say, "All men have been my mothers, and all women have been my fathers." The meaning here is that beings now reborn as men could have been born in past lives as women, and were my mothers. And she could later be reborn as a man. The essay simply outlines these principles, and we ourselves can fill in all the details.

Not only people have been my parents, but those now reborn as horses, cows, sheep, chickens, and other animals all have family ties with us. But we turn our backs on becoming enlightened and mix with the defiling dust; we fail to recognize such relations. Thus, we make an enemy of someone who is clearly a father or a mother to us.

"We whip the mule until it bleeds; who could know that it is our mother in anguish?" Although it is now a mule, it was, in lives past, my mother. She was reborn, according to her offenses, as a mule. And we don't recognize her, and pick up a whip to strike the animal when it gets lazy and won't work hard. But every time we strike it, our mother from a past life is unbearably pained to the point of tears. Pigs, dogs, and all living beings have been in my family; we all immigrate to different species, looking for a new "house" to live in. And "from out of the belly of a horse, we enter the womb of a mule. How many times have we been through King Yama's court? We fall from Shakra's palace, back into Yama's pot." After being born in Lord Shakra's heaven, we are reborn again, and fall into King Yama's pot of boiling oil. People like to go on vacation and travel, so too do our souls, thinking that it is such fun to roam about.

Sometimes we roam about and end up in peaceful surroundings, like in a luxury hotel. There is a hot bath, and a soft bed to relax on. We banker for these luxuries, and like to eat well too. But we end up going down the wrong road due to our liking these luxuries; we like gourmet dishes made with mutton, beef, and pork and prepared in many fancy ways. But after we eat those animals' flesh, we must repay our blood debt to them. If you take another's money, you must repay that money. If you take another's flesh for food, you also must repay that debt. And having eaten quite a lot of others' flesh, people can't fail to repay their debts. They will be reborn as a pig, duck, or other animal in order to repay those debts.

There was a case in point in America; a businessman sold chickens, tens of thousands daily. He looked much like a chicken himself. He might have been a chicken in past lives, and along with his flock was eaten by people. Now, he is a human, and past chicken eaters are now reborn as chickens. Now he kills them for food. He supplied them with nutrition in the past, and now they supply him with nutrition in this life. They nourish their present causes and future retributions together. Just look at sheep ranchers; they look like sheep. They might have been sheep in past lives, and been eaten by others. Now in this life they want revenge. Look at how very bovine the eyes of a cattle rancher are! Fish mongers resemble fish. You aren't paying attention if you haven't noticed this yet. Whoever now is selling the flesh of any other being was probably just that species of being itself in its past life, now reborn a human, looking for revenge. The net of karma is just this constricting.

Yet this net of karma catches us in other ways, too. If someone loves her dog, that dog might be reborn a human, as a handsome man, who then gets married to his previous owner. In my home town, there was a man who was an actor, an opera singer, in his past life. He was reborn good-looking in this life, but his bride was homely; she was once a dog in the opera troupe. Now as his wife, she continued to yelp all day, and argue with her husband. He couldn't find a moment's peace, and didn't know what to do about his plight. Our past roles and habits, no matter what they are, continue in this life. So we shouldn't feel elated and proud of being human now, doing as we please, thus, ending up confused and upside down.

"We whip the mule until it bleeds; who could know that it is our mother in anguish?" Who could know that the mule he is beating was once his own mother in a past life? Now she is pained beyond her limits.

We lead the pig to slaughter; who could know that it is our father in agony? Dragging the pig by a rope to the butcher's block, the farmer doesn't know it is his own father in a past life. He simply thinks the pig is fat enough for market; and butchers it. His father, however, is wracked with pain. **We eat our own sons without being aware, just like King Wen.** King Wen was once in custody. His enemies, wishing to test the rumors that the king had supernatural powers, killed one of the king's sons, cooked his flesh, and served it to the king, to see if he would know what was happening. He ate it. If he knew it was his son, he wouldn't have eaten it. Some people say that he knew, but ate it all the same, to make others think he didn't know. But no, if he knew, he wouldn't have eaten. He, through ignorance, made many mistakes, and so do we. Girlfriends don't see that their boyfriends were once their grandfathers, uncles, fathers – it is not for sure who they are. All they see is how young and handsome they are; they quickly set out to snare them. They catch their man, but the whole scene is upside-down. They get everything all confused. Even someone as brilliant and virtuous as King Wen didn't recognize his past relatives.

And we gulp down our own relatives without recognizing them. This is the way of all ordinary people. Day in and day out, ordinary people are like this. They eat their past fathers and mothers, their grandparents, their own flesh and blood. And they don't even know. Most are like this, none escape the cycle of cause and effect. **The loved ones of yesteryear are now sworn enemies.** The close relatives we cherished and loved in past lives may have now become horses or cows. We dine on their flesh.

"Fine," they say. "You eat me now, how heartless! I'll gnaw your bones next time around!" And the ties of vengeance are knotted as they swear to get even. Hated **rivals of days past are now our blood relatives.** Some families don't get along. **Our mothers of past lives are our wives of the present. Our fathers-in-law of old are now our husbands.** We feel close to them, but don't see the past ties and reasons why. So now, we become lost and muddled in the shuffle of ensuing rebirths, and everything becomes confused.

Those with knowledge of past lives recognize these changes; they feel shame and embarrassment. They are ashamed, how could they hold their heads up when they know what is really happening? **Those with the Heavenly Eye see these situations; they find them ridiculous and pathetic.**

In the cycle of rebirth, as babies, **amid excrement and filth, we pass nine difficult months** in the womb. **We emerge from the path of pus and blood in a pitiable state.** The baby is born upside down and is a piteous sight. **When young, we know nothing and cannot tell east from west.** Kids have no education; they don't know anything at all. **As adults, we become more aware, but our greed and desire arise.** Adults have received an education, but what do they know? They don't know about the paying of debts involved in the cycle of cause and effect; they focus their attention on lust. Women want only to catch a man, and men chase after women. For some, the stakes are so high that they end it all if they don't get what they want. They are so confused that they fail to recognize that in reality it is all very pointless.

In an instant, after the very short time we have in this life, **old age and illness overtake us.** No girls will want you when you become old and wrinkled. They will see you are old and gray and they won't want you. In fact, husbands nowadays leave their aging wives and find younger women. The world is getting worse everyday. If you can see through all this, then stop being so confused in your behaviour and put it all down! **Suddenly death arrives.** Death is as swift as a wild grass fire; it overtakes us quickly.

Amid the blaze of wind and fire, two of the four elements get out of balance. The wind fans the fires to reach a heat of thousands of degrees, burning things to a crisp. **Our spirit becomes disordered,** and we lose all correct feeling in our bodies, and lose our powers to reason and become oblivious to everything. **Our vital energies and blood are exhausted.** Thus marriage leads one to an early death. The two fear living to a ripe old age, and wish to die sooner. Girls find boyfriends, saying, "Help me die sooner, I don't want to live." Men, looking for a way to die, find girlfriends saying, "Help me die sooner!" Together they get involved in love – the road to death! To live we must have our reproductive essence, our breath, and our spirit. Without our reproductive essence, we die. And we obviously can't live if our breath is cut off. And our spirit is our awareness and consciousness. We live because our reproductive essence and breath are intact. Living recklessly, we end up devouring our own essential energies. Those who are casual and lax and take delight in a bohemian life-style are seriously upside down.

"But what you are talking about will mean the end of the human race," someone may object. Not really, because there is no way that all people will understand or agree with this. No matter how you explain the dangers involved, they still want to tread that path. "It's a dead-end road," you say, but they answer, "I'll just try it out and see." Due to this deeply rooted confusion, it is not easy to get people to wake up. But I'll do my best to tell you all now.

Our flesh and skin wither and dry up. When our reproductive essence, our breath, and our spirit are gone, the skin and flesh dry out. The elements return to their respective origins; what is earth goes back to the earth, what is liquid goes back to the water element, wind goes to wind and fire to fire. The four elements break up. **We feel as if iron needles are piercing our every pore and as if knives are hacking our every orifice.** At death's door, we feel as if every pore is being reamed by needles. Our essence, energy, and spirit are gone, and our every bodily orifice is pained as if hacked by knives.

When the spirit leaves the body at death, it feels more pain than does a live turtle having its shell ripped off before it is thrown in the pot. The turtle undergoes excruciating pain, but the spirit leaving the body at death is even more painful!

The Suffering in Birth and Death

Essay:

The mind has no fixed purpose. It flits hurriedly from place to place like a traveling peddler. Our bodies have no fixed shapes. We continually exchange them as if we were moving from room to room in a house. We have had and lost more bodies than there are particles of dust in a billion worlds. We have cried more tears at parting than all the water in the billows of the four seas. The stacks of bones rise higher than mountain peaks. The heaps of corpses are vaster than the earth.

If the Buddha had not spoken of this, who would have recognized or even imagined these things? If we do not read the Buddha's sutras, how can we know and be aware of these truths? If we continue our hankering for love and pleasure, we will forever remain stupid and confused.

Then the grave concern is that one mistake has led to another for ten thousand kalpas, through thousands of lives. A human body is hard to obtain and easy to lose. Good times soon pass and cannot be brought back. The road is dark and gloomy, and separations last a long time. I must endure evil retribution in the Three Paths alone. The pain is unspeakable; who would stand in for me? Even discussing this subject chills my heart.

We, therefore, must halt the flow of birth and death, get out of the ocean of love and desire, save ourselves and save others, and together reach the other shore. Of all things from the beginning of time onward, this is the most extraordinary achievement, yet one only needs to begin.

This is the sixth cause and condition for making the resolve to attain Bodhi.

Commentary:

The mind has no fixed purpose. People have difficulty making their own decisions, and be decisive about things. If people could make their own decisions, then they would never do any false thinking. But because the human mind has no fixed purpose, **it flits hurriedly from place to place like a traveling peddler.** Someone who hawks his wares, hurries here and there, unlike a shopkeeper who has a shop. **Our bodies have no fixed shapes.** This life we're tall, last life we were short. This body is not really us; the body is like a house. Thus there is a poem:

> We pass our lives like staying in a room,
> The mouth is the door,
> Windows are the eyes, ears, and nose.
> The limbs are the pillars,
> The hair is the thatched roof.
> Always keep the house in good repair,
> Don't wait until it falls down
> And then try to patch it up.

Don't let your house go to ruin; you'll panic and fret, looking for a new place. Our bodies are like houses, and the owner is inside. Who is the owner? The owner is the mind. But the mind can't take charge; it doesn't make the decisions. Instead, it follows what the unseen forces like ghosts tell it to do, and engages in false thinking. It is moved by external objects. Thus, the mind "flits hurriedly from place to place," and "our bodies have no fixed shapes." **We**

continually exchange them as if we were moving from room to room in a house. After staying long enough in that old, cold house, our mind moves to another. From a small thatched hut in this life, it moves to a high-rise condominium in its next life. **We have had and lost more bodies than there are particles of dust in a billion worlds.** We go, then return, go, then return, countless many times. **We have cried more tears at parting than all the water in the billows of the four seas.** The waters of the oceans is unfathomable, but the tears we have cried when leaving or reuniting with relatives are even more. **The stacks of bones rise higher than mountain peaks. The heaps of corpses are more vaster the earth,** more in number than blades of grass in a field.

If the Buddha had not spoken of this, and if we had had no way to know what he said, **who would have recognized or even imagined these things?** Who could know? No one. **If we do not read the Buddha's sutras, how can we know and be aware of these truths? If we continue our hankering for love and pleasure,** if people continue to be greedy for and love such stinking skin bags, **we will forever remain stupid and confused,** failing to understand the doctrines just discussed. If we never realize what's being said, then **the grave concern is that one mistake has led to another for ten thousand kalpas, through thousands of lives. A human body is hard to obtain,** so now, while we are in human bodies we should use the opportunity well, since they are **easy to lose. Good times,** when we are young, **soon pass and cannot be brought back.** You'll never get your prime of life back, no matter how much you want to.

The road is dark and gloomy, it's hard to see anything, **and separations last a long time. I must endure evil retribution in the Three Paths,** the hells, hungry ghosts, and animals, **alone.** You planted the evil causes, and the evil retributions are yours. **The pain is unspeakable; who would stand in for me? Who would take the evil punishment for me?** Who would take the evil punishment for me? **Even discussing this subject** is frightening and **chills my heart.**

We, therefore, must halt the flow of birth and death, cultivate with the intent of quickly ending birth and death, **get out of the ocean,** the sea of suffering of **love and desire, save ourselves and save others.** May we all leave suffering and reach bliss, and are saved, **and together reach the other shore. Of all things from the beginning of time onward,** throughout the countless kalpas past, **this** matter of ending birth and death **is the most extraordinary achievement,** the greatest work that can be done. **Yet,** it's right here that one must end birth and death, and **one only needs to begin.**

This is the sixth cause and condition for making the resolve to attain Bodhi. This is the sixth crucial reason explaining why we absolutely must develop the resolve to attain Bodhi.

Reverence of the Spiritual Nature

Essay:

What is reverence for our own spiritual nature? It is that in the present, single thought, I can immediately be one with the Thus Come One, Shakyamuni, without any difference at all. Why is it, then, that the World Honored One realized proper enlightenment an infinite number of kalpas ago, yet we are still muddled, confused, and upside down? Why are we still only ordinary people?

The Buddha, the World Honored One, has also perfected infinite spiritual penetrations, wisdom, and the adornments of merit and virtue, while we only have an infinite number of karmic ties and afflictions and are bound to birth and death. Our minds and natures and his are one, but our confusion and his enlightenment are as far apart as the sky and the abysmal deeps. In stillness, contemplate this matter: how can we not be ashamed?

It is as if we had dropped a priceless pearl into a mud puddle, considering it as worthless as a broken tile, neither cherishing nor esteeming it. We should, therefore, use an infinite number of wholesome methods to serve as antidotes to our afflictions. By cultivating virtue, we gain merit, and the virtue of our nature can then appear. Thus we wash the pearl and set it up high, where it releases a penetrating radiance that outshines everything. Then we can say that we have not been ungrateful to the Buddha's teaching and have not failed to uncover our own spiritual nature.

This is the seventh cause and condition for making the resolve to attain Bodhi.

Commentary:

What is reverence for our own spiritual nature? We must revere our spiritual nature, our Buddha nature, our magical nature. This nature is the same in the Buddha as it is in all living beings. Why, then, does the Buddha have such great wisdom? And why are all living beings so stupid? The Buddha has cultivated virtue, and thus has merit. Thus, "the merit of his nature then appears," as the text states later on. And thus the Buddha's natural wisdom of our basic nature appears. But if you fail to cultivate, then your basic nature won't show through, even though it is there.

A table, for example, is latent in a tree. The tree grows tall, is felled and milled into boards, and is made into a table. We can't use the tree as a table. It can only be called a tree. It can be used to construct many different useful pieces of furniture. If you lack the appropriate skills to work with the wood, however, you might only be able to make firewood out of it.

Our spiritual nature is the same. If you can use it, the light of wisdom will appear. If you can't, you will be the people who don't recognize the worth of a tree, and cut it up for firewood. Thus they pass through many births and deaths without end.

One main difference between Buddhism and other religions is found here. Other religions say that there are certain limits that people have, certain things they cannot do. The Buddha, however, teaches us the way to open our inherent wisdom. Anyone who can open up his wisdom can become a Buddha. And becoming a Buddha is done by following these six principles: not fighting, not being greedy, not seeking, not being selfish, not wanting personal advantage, and not lying. It is just this simple. Follow these six principles, and you are a Buddha. But people don't follow them. They may say, "I'll not fight," but they argue with the next person who comes along. They may say, "I'll stop being greedy." But they are first to grab for the goods when they see a chance. They may say that they don't seek for things, but when they feel that they need something, they still seek for whatever it is. They may say that they are not selfish and don't want personal advantages, but things happen and they are very self-centered when it comes to big, important matters. Last is lying. People don't even need to learn how to lie; they are naturally good at it. Some people even lie, then claim that what they said was "expedient speech, suited to the situation at the time." You are not far from Buddhahood if you can thoroughly follow these six principles.

How should we revere our spiritual nature? By not looking lightly on it. Don't waste it. It can be made into valuable Buddha altars, tables, and the like. Don't burn it up as firewood; it will be left a worthless pile of ashes. This is the seventh reason we should resolve on Bodhi. Respect yourself and your inherent wisdom. Don't take yourself lightly.

It is that in the present, single thought, the single thought is the nature, **I can immediately be one with the Thus Come One, Shakyamuni, without any difference at all.** The Buddha became a Buddha by means of his nature and mind. We, too, can become Buddhas by means of our spiritual natures and minds; thus the minds and natures are "without any difference at all." But **why is it, then, that the World Honored One realized proper enlightenment an infinite number of kalpas ago,** becoming a Buddha, **yet we are still muddled, confused, and upside down? Why are we still only** unenlightened **ordinary people?**

The Buddha, the World Honored One, has also perfected infinite spiritual penetrations, the six penetrations: the heavenly ear to hear what the gods are saying, the heavenly eye to see all the activities in the heavens, knowledge of others' thoughts to know what others are thinking, the knowledge of past lives to know at a glance whether someone was once a cow, a horse, a pig, an ant, a mosquito, or a person, and the Buddha can see all past lives, knowing how many times someone has been any number of beings, the ending of outflows, and the complete spirit.

The Buddha has the three bodies, too: the dharma body, the reward body, and the transformation body. **Wisdom,** the four kinds of wisdom: the level and equal wisdom, the wonderful contemplating wisdom, the wisdom to get things done, and the perfect mirror wisdom. The Buddha also has the five eyes: the Buddha eye, the dharma eye, the wisdom eye, the heavenly eye, and the form eye.

How does the Buddha have such spiritual penetrations and wisdom? They are due to **the adornments of merit and virtue.** He has sufficient merit and virtue. **While we only have an infinite number of karmic ties** binding us up and many **afflictions and are bound to birth and death.** Being born then dying, being born again and then dying, over and over, we never get free of it. **Our minds and natures and his are one,** the Buddhas' mind and nature is the same as ours, **but our confusion and his enlightenment are as far apart as the sky and the abysmal depths.** But the Buddha is enlightened, and can properly use it. We are still confused; thus we are as far apart as a deep abyss is far from the heavens. **In stillness, contemplate this matter**: be calm and think clearly, **how can we not be ashamed?** The Buddha has already become a Buddha and open his great wisdom; we are still so muddled and confused. We are not great heroes, great gladiators, or great victors. We are very pitiable and shameful.

It is as if we had dropped a priceless pearl, our spiritual nature is like a priceless jewel, **into a mud puddle,** into dung or manure, **considering it as worthless as a broken tile, neither cherishing nor esteeming it,** our spiritual nature. **We should, therefore, use an infinite number of wholesome methods to serve as antidotes to our afflictions.** If a person has sufficient merit and virtue, he or she can be reborn in the heavens. But if we've accumulated enough offenses and transgressions, we will fall into the hells. We should, therefore, stop doing evil and respectfully do all good. When we have enough merit and virtue, our afflictions will naturally disappear. **By cultivating virtue,** we gain merit, successfully doing good for a long enough time **the virtue of our nature can then appear.** The merit and virtue of our nature will appear, as will our wisdom.

Thus we wash the pearl and set it up high, where it releases a penetrating radiance that outshines everything. Then we can say that we have not been ungrateful to the Buddha's teaching and have not failed to uncover our own spiritual nature.

This is the seventh cause and condition for making the resolve to attain Bodhi. Don't forget it! Don't waste your spiritual nature!

Repenting of Karmic Obstacles

Essay:

What is repenting of karmic obstacles and reforming? The sutras say that a precept holder who commits one duskrita will fall into the Nirtaka Hell for a period equal to a five-hundred-year lifespan in the Heaven of Four Kings. Duskrita are small offenses, yet precept holders who commit them will receive such retribution. Serious offenses evoke even more suffering; the retribution they bring is indescribable.

We constantly break the precepts by everything we do in our daily lives. With each meal we take and with each drop we drink, we transgress the sila. A single day's transgressions are beyond reckoning. How much more numerous are the transgressions committed during kalpa after kalpa! They are indescribably many.

Moreover, it is said, "Of ten people who receive the Five Precepts nine will transgress them." Few admit their errors; most conceal them. The Five Precepts are the Upasaka Precepts; yet we fail to perfectly uphold even these, not to mention the Shramanera, Bhikshu, and Bodhisattva Precepts.

If you ask our titles, we will reply, "We are Bhikshus." But in fact, we do not even come up to being Upasakas. How can we fail to be ashamed?

We should know that receiving the precepts set forth by the Buddhas is the choice of the individual. If we have received them, we must not transgress them. If we do not transgress them, we have no need for concern. Transgress them, and in the end we will certainly fall.

If we fail to have pity on ourselves and others, if we fail to have compassion for ourselves and for others, if we fail to be harmonious and sincere in word and deed, if we fail to sigh and weep, if we fail to painfully seek repentance and reform together with all living beings everywhere, then our evil retributions due from thousands of lifetimes throughout tens of thousands of kalpas will be difficult to escape.

This is the eighth cause and condition for making the resolve to attain Bodhi.

Commentary:

What is repenting of karmic obstacles and reforming? "Repenting" is to repent of past errors. "Reforming" is to refrain from future violations. The power of repentance and reform is inconceivable. The sutras say about the Precepts and the Vinaya **that a precept holder who commits one duskrita will fall into the Nirtaka Hell for a period equal to a five-hundred-year lifespan in the Heavens of Four Kings.** A "duskrita" is a minor defiling offense, a mistake that is light; it causes a small defilement. Yet a precept holder who commits one duskrita, one must undergo retribution in the hells for a period of time equal to five hundred years in the Heavens of the Four Kings. Then the offense can be wiped away. **Duskrita are small offenses, yet precept holders who commit them will receive such retribution. Serious offenses evoke even more suffering.** How much the more severe are heavy and grave offenses like the Parajikas, the ten major offenses or the Sanghavashesha offenses – the heavy offenses. **The retribution they bring is indescribable.** It is even more difficult to know the extent of the retribution one must undergo for one's heavy offenses.

We constantly break the precepts by everything we do in our daily lives. At present, we monastics constantly violate the precepts and the Vinaya in our four deportments of walking, standing, sitting, and reclining, as well as in our every movement and action, in every word and deed of our daily lives, and with the things we use everyday. **With each meal we take and with each drop we drink, we transgress the sila. We are not in accord with the Precepts or with the Vinaya.**

A single day's transgressions are beyond reckoning. The transgressions of a single day are measureless and boundless in number. **How much more numerous are the transgressions committed during kalpa after kalpa!** So much more are the offenses committed in each life throughout such a long time! **They are indescribably many** – even less can we know their number.

Moreover, it is said, "Of ten people who receive the Five Precepts nine will transgress them." Nine out of ten people who receive the Five Precepts violate them. Few admit their errors; most conceal them. They transgress the precepts and do not admit it, or repent and reform. They conceal their errors in their hearts and think nobody knows. **The Five Precepts are** called **the Upasaka Precepts** and are received by lay people, the male upasakas and the female upasikas. **Yet we fail to perfectly uphold even these.** We do not cultivate them. Monastics are included among those who transgress the Five Precepts; they hold them imperfectly, incompletely. **Not to mention the Shramanera, Bhikshu, and Bodhisattva Precepts.** Certainly the Ten Shramanera, the Two Hundred Fifty Bhikshu, and the Ten Major and Forty-eight Minor Bodhisattva Precepts are often transgressed.

If you ask a fully-ordained monastic his title, he will reply that he is a Bhikshu. "Bhikshu" has three meanings:

1. Mendicant
2. Frightener of Mara
3. Destroyer of evil

As a mendicant, one beseeches the Dharma from all Buddhas above, and below, one receives alms-food from living beings. As a frightener of Mara, the novice is asked by the Karmadana during the transmission of the Bhikshu precepts, "Are you a great hero?" "Yes, I am a great hero," answers the preceptee, whereupon the palaces of the heavenly demons tremble and shake; the demon king is frightened and thinks, "The retinue of Shakyamuni Buddha has increased and my horde of demons has decreased." The thought scares him, so the Bhikshu has frightened Mara. As a destroyer of evil, one destroys the evil afflictions of greed, hatred, and stupidity.

But in fact, if asked truly and genuinely, **we do not even come up to being Upasakas.** Some monks and nuns, however, are genuinely lofty and pure in their deportment of upholding the precepts and truly are models for gods and people. **How can we fail to be shamed?** People who have left home and become monastics but who do not even meet the standards for laypeople should be deeply ashamed.

We should know that receiving the precepts set forth by the Buddhas is the choice of the individual. If we have received them, we must not transgress them, as

> When living beings receive the Buddhas' precepts,
> They enter the Buddha's position.
> When their state is identical to Great Enlightenment,
> They are truly the Buddha's disciples.
>
> Brahma Net Sutra

After receiving the Buddhas' precepts, one must uphold them. **If we do not transgress them, we have no need for concern,** and, there is no problem. **Transgress them, and in the end we will certainly fall.** In the future, anyone who makes the transgressions will certainly fall.

If we fail to have pity on ourselves and others, to have sympathy for ourselves and for other people, **if we fail to have**

compassion for ourselves and for others, to be grieved for ourselves and for others; **if we fail to be harmonious and sincere in word and deed,** to keep body, mouth and mind concentrated; **if we fail to sigh and weep,** to let our tears fall when repenting before the Buddhas; and **if we fail to painfully seek repentance and reform together with all living beings everywhere** before the Buddhas, **then our evil retributions due from thousands of lifetimes throughout tens of thousands of kalpas** – from measureless kalpas past onwards – **will be difficult to escape.** If we do not repent and reform, we will have to undergo our evil retribution; it is difficult to avoid and must be undergone unless we truly, genuinely repent and reform.

This is the eighth cause and condition for making the resolve to attain Bodhi.

Rebirth in the Pure Land

Essay:

What is the wish for rebirth in the Pure Land? Progress on the spiritual Path is difficult when we cultivate in this world. But once we have been reborn in that land, becoming a Buddha is easy. Because cultivating is easy there, we can be successful in a single lifetime. Because it is difficult here, many kalpas have passed and we still have not accomplished our goal. Therefore, each and every sage and worthy of the past has taken the path that leads to that land. And passage after passage in all the thousands of sutras and myriads of shastras points in this direction. For cultivators in the Dharma Ending Age, nothing surpasses this method.

The sutra says, however, that we cannot be reborn there if our good deeds are few. Only through many acts deserving of blessings can we be successful. They say that none of the many acts deserving of blessings equals maintaining mindfulness of Amitabha Buddha's name. They say that none of the many good deeds equals a great resolution of the mind. Therefore, reciting the Sage's name even briefly is superior to practicing giving for a hundred years. And by simply making the great resolve, we transcend kalpa after kalpa of cultivation.

Thus, we may practice mindfulness of the Buddha with the hope of becoming Buddhas, but if we fail to make the great resolve, our mindfulness will not be sincere. We may be determined to cultivate, but retreat is easy, despite our resolve, unless we are reborn in the Pure Land.

Therefore, plant a Bodhi seed. Till with the plow of mindfulness of the Buddha, and the fruits of the Path will naturally grow. Sail the ship of great vows to enter the ocean of the Pure Land. Then we will certainly be reborn in the West.

This is the ninth cause and condition for making the resolve to attain Bodhi.

Commentary:

What is the wish for rebirth in the Pure Land? Why should we want to be reborn in the Pure Land? Progress in the Path is difficult when we cultivate in this world, the Saha world. Although we can cultivate here, it is very difficult to make constant, daily progress. But once we have been reborn in that land, the Land of Ultimate Bliss, becoming a Buddha is easy. "When the flower blooms, we see the Buddha, and awaken to the patience in which no phenomena arise." Because cultivating is easy there in the Pure Land, we can be successful in a single lifetime. Because it is difficult here in the Saha world, many kalpas have passed and we still have not accomplished our goal. Therefore, each and every sage and worthy of the past has taken the path that leads to this land. All the patriarchs and worthies of the past sought to be reborn in the Pure Land. And passage after passage in all the thousands of sutras spoken by the Buddha and myriads of shastras written by the patriarchs, as well as all Vinaya texts, points in this direction. The main import of any of these texts is to instruct us to seek to be reborn in the Pure Land. For cultivators in the Dharma Ending Age, like us now, nothing surpasses this method. The Pure Land method is the easiest and most direct of all the Dharma doors.

The *Amitabha Sutra* **says, however, that we cannot be reborn there if our good deeds are few.** The *Amitabha Sutra* says, "Shariputra, one cannot have few good roots, blessings, virtues, and causal connections to attain birth in that land." **Only through many acts deserving of blessings can we be successful.** You need to do more good deeds to gain more blessings. **They say that none of the many acts deserving of blessings equals maintaining mindfulness of Amitabha Buddha's name.** How can you do more blessed deeds? Simply by reciting the Buddha's name, you can be doing blessed deeds and increasing your blessings and virtue. **They say that none of the many good deeds equals a great resolution of the mind.** How can you do good deeds? Simply by making the great resolve upon Bodhi. **Therefore, reciting the Sage's,** Amitabha Buddha's, **name even briefly is superior to practicing giving for a hundred years.** Reciting the Buddha's name for a short while is better than making gifts of the seven kinds of jewels for a hundred years. **And by simply making the great resolve, we transcend kalpa after kalpa,** kalpas as many as particles of dust, **of cultivation.**

Thus, we may practice mindfulness of the Buddha with the hope of becoming Buddhas, but if we fail to make the great resolve, our mindfulness will not be sincere. The reason we are mindful of the Buddha is that we wish to become Buddhas. If you don't want to become a Buddha, you don't need to be mindful of the Buddha. But if you don't make a great resolve to attain Bodhi, you won't have any reason to be mindful of the Buddha, and your mindfulness and recitation will be aimless. **We may be determined to cultivate,** we may be determined to practice, **but retreat is easy, despite our resolve, unless we are reborn in the Pure Land.**

Therefore, plant a Bodhi seed by making a vast, great resolve. **Till with the plow of mindfulness of the Buddha,** like tilling the soil, **and the fruits of the Path will naturally grow.** As you recite, a lotus will sprout in the Western Land of Ultimate Bliss. **Sail the ship of great vows to enter the ocean of the Pure Land. Then we**

will certainly be reborn in the West, by being mindful of Amitabha Buddha.

This is the ninth cause and condition for making the resolve to attain Bodhi.

The Proper Dharma

Essay:

What is the wish to cause the Proper Dharma to remain long in the world? Our World Honored One, for our sakes, cultivated the Bodhi Path for an infinite number of kalpas. He could practice what was difficult to practice and could endure what was difficult to endure. His causes were perfect, his results were complete; thus, he became a Buddha. After becoming a Buddha, he finished teaching those with whom he had affinities, and then he entered Nirvana.

The Proper Dharma Age and Dharma Semblance Age have already ended. Now we are in the Dharma Ending Age; there are teachings but no adherents. No one can distinguish the deviant from the proper; no one can tell right from wrong. We compete and struggle with each other. We pursue fame and fortune. Look around: the deluge has spread throughout the world.

No one knows who the Buddha is, what the Dharma means, or what constitutes the Sangha. The decay has reached such a perilous point that one can scarcely bear to speak of it. Every time I consider it, my tears fall without my realizing it. I am a disciple of the Buddha, yet I am unable to return the kindness that has been done for me. I do not benefit myself; I cannot benefit others. While alive, I am of no benefit to my time. After death, I will be of no benefit to posterity. Although the heavens are high, they cannot cover me. Although the earth is thick, it cannot bear me. If my own offenses are not extremely grave, then whose are?

Commentary:

What is the wish to cause the Proper Dharma to remain long in the world? How can we cause the Proper Dharma to remain in this world and not die out in this world? **Our World Honored One,** Shakyamuni Buddha, **for our sakes,** the Buddha wished to cultivate and become a Buddha so that he could pull us out of the suffering we are in. He wanted us to be able to end birth and death and get out of the cycle of the revolving wheel; thus he **cultivated the Bodhi Path for an infinite number of kalpas** up to this day. The Buddha cultivated blessings and wisdom for three great asamkhyeya kalpas, planting the causes for his majestic appearance. "Asamkhyeya" is Sanskrit, meaning "an uncountable number," and is one of the six great numbers. Three innumerably long kalpas is a long time indeed! In such a long time, wishing to teach and transform living beings, to resolve upon Bodhi, and to cultivate to become a Buddha, the Buddha gave away his body and life, and was born again, over and over, in every square inch of this world. For example, he fed his body to a starving tigress. The Buddha saw her on the brink of starvation and gave her his own body. Who could make such a sacrifice? Most people want to live and fear death; rarely is anyone willing to forsake his own well-being in order to secure the life of another. Throughout three uncountably long kalpas, the Buddha gave away his own life in order to help us living beings; therefore, we should repay the Buddha's kindness. We might have once eaten the Buddha's flesh or drank his blood. Now that we are of the Buddhist faith, we should do a good job of repaying the Buddha's kindness. We should be thankful, because the Buddha gave us his life so that we could live. **He could practice what was difficult** for most ordinary people **to practice.** This means doing things like giving to others his head, eyes, brains, and marrow. Someone might need eyes, and he gave them his. He didn't wait until after he died to donate them, he made a gift of them while he was living. Someone might have needed brains to cure an illness; he gave them his, and gave up his life to save another. He also could have given away the marrow of his bones to save someone's life.

In his many different lives, he was able to give up his country, city, wife, and children. He yielded the throne to his heir, thus giving away his country. Or he gave away his wealth and riches, thus giving away his city. The most difficult thing for most men to give up is their wife and family, the Buddha gave them to others. The Buddha was able to give away both inner and outer wealth to help others who needed them. No one can match the Buddha's selfless spirit of sacrifice for others.

And could endure what was difficult for most people **to endure. His causes were perfect, his results were complete; thus, he became a Buddha.** The seeds he planted were perfect and so the results they brought were complete; he became a Buddha. **After becoming a Buddha, he finished teaching those with whom he had affinities,** he taught the living beings who were ready to be taught, **and then he entered Nirvana.** What is "Nirvana?" It is the state when nothing comes into being, and nothing ceases to be. You don't undergo birth and death, but have ended birth and death.

The Proper Dharma Age occurs when a Buddha lives in the world, people cultivate, have Chan samadhi, and become sages **and Dharma Semblance Age** occurs when people don't really cultivate, but simply put on a false show. In the Proper Dharma Age, people meditate and can enter samadhi. In the Dharma Semblance Age, people work on superficial things like building temples and making Buddha images. These two ages last a thousand years each, and they **have already ended. Now we are** already **in the Dharma Ending Age,** where it is as though we are but grasping at branch tips. The Proper Dharma Age is like being at the roots and trunk of the tree; and the Dharma Semblance Age is like being at the upper trunk of the tree. The Dharma Ending Age lasts ten thousand years. We still have more than nine thousand years left. When people truly cultivate during the Dharma Ending Age there is a Proper Age within the Dharma Ending Age. And there is a Semblance Age in the Dharma Ending Age when people build temples or make Buddha images during the Dharma Ending Age. But the Dharma Ending Age exists for those who neither cultivate nor make images, and the sutras will disappear by themselves. They will disappear until only the *Amitabha Sutra* is left. It will then last for five hundred years and then disappear, too. Only Amitabha Buddha's name will remain for a hundred years, saving countless living beings, then the Dharma will disappear from this world.

Then, no one will know about reciting the Buddha's name or about any Dharma at all. Although we are now in the Dharma Ending Age, times are still good enough that we can work hard at cultivating.

In the Dharma Ending Age, **there are teachings but no adherents.** They will directly oppose the Buddhas' teachings. Monks and nuns do not eat meat, drink liquor, or chase women, but as the Dharma disappears, they will. The teachings will exist, but no one will really cultivate. What will ensue? **No one can distinguish the deviant** – the self-claimed sages, and the monastics who don't do what monastics should do – **from the proper.** People will not recognize externalist sects, but will believe what they say. **No one can tell right from wrong. We compete and struggle with each other. We pursue fame and fortune,** name and gain are the only goals. **Look around: the deluge has spread throughout the world.** Just look at the world; everyone is caught up in getting fame and fortune. Monastics studying here who want fame and fortune must change, and become real cultivators.

No one knows who the Buddha is, or what he was about, **what the Dharma means,** in that it teaches us to stop doing any evil, become good, and to understand the truth. Instead, they will become more stupid and confused as they continue to study. **Or what constitutes the Sangha.** What is the Sangha? The Buddha, the Dharma, and the Sangha are the Triple Jewel. "Sangha" means a group of four or more monks living in harmony together, not one person living on his own. **The decay has reached such a perilous point** that people cannot even identify the Buddha, the Dharma, or the Sangha. **One can scarcely bear to speak of it.** It is unspeakable. **Every time I consider it, my tears fall like rain without my realizing it. I am a disciple of the Buddha,** a left-home person, **yet I am unable to return the kindness that have been done for me** by the Buddha. **I do not benefit myself;** I've not done a good job of cultivating, and thus have not helped myself, **I cannot benefit others** around me. **While alive, I am of no benefit to my time. After death, I will be of no benefit to posterity. Although the heavens are high, they cannot cover me. Although the earth is thick, it cannot bear me.** I have done nothing to merit the earth's support and the heaven's cover. **If my own offenses are not extremely grave, then whose are?** I'm the most rotten; I should be very ashamed and should make the great resolve to attain Bodhi.

Essay:

My pain is, therefore, unbearable. I have no recourse but to immediately forget my baseness and quickly make the great resolve. Although I cannot reverse the fate of the Dharma's end in the present, I certainly must plan to protect and uphold the Proper Dharma in the future.

Therefore good friends, gather together at the Way Place, perform the Karmavachana, and establish Dharma assemblies. Make the forty-eight vows; make vow after vow to save living beings. Make a deep resolve that will last for hundreds of thousands of kalpas; in thought after thought, resolve to be a Buddha.

From this day to the end of future time, vow to return to the peace of the Pure Land at the end of every life, to ascend to the nine grades of lotuses, and to then come back to the Saha World. Make the Buddhas' sun gloriously shine once more. Open the gate of the Dharma again. Let the ocean of the Sangha be clear and pure in this world. The people of the east will be taught and the kalpa will be prolonged. The Proper Dharma will long continue. Such is the meager but genuine resolve I strive to fulfill.

This is the tenth cause and condition for making the resolve to attain Bodhi.

Commentary:

My pain is, therefore, unbearable, referring to the reasons in the previous section. **I have no recourse,** there is nothing else I can do **but to immediately forget my baseness and quickly make the great resolve.** I won't wallow in self-pity, feeling that I am worthless and unsavable, but instead I'll resolve to spread the Buddha's teaching so it flourishes, thus saving living beings. **Although I cannot reverse the fate of the Dharma's end in the present,** and wipe out the rotten trends in the world now, but I will do all I can, hoping that at least one person will turn over a new leaf and return to his basic purity. **I certainly must plan to protect and uphold the Proper Dharma in the future.** That is why the great Master wrote this essay for us now, so that we will learn of the way things are, and resolve upon Bodhi.

Therefore good friends, my fellow meditators and friends in the spiritual Path, **gather together at the Way Place, perform the Karmavachana,** and repentance ceremonies **and establish Dharma assemblies. Make the forty-eight vows**; like the forty-eight vows of Amitabha Buddha, **make vow after vow to save living beings. Make a deep resolve that will last for hundreds of thousands of kalpas**; hoping to develop the seeds of Bodhi that have been buried deep inside for a long time. **In thought after thought, resolve to be a Buddha.**

From this day to the end of future time, vow to return to the peace of the Pure Land at the end of every life, to ascend to the nine grades of lotuses, and to then come back to the Saha World. Make the Buddhas' sun gloriously shine once more. Open the gate of the Dharma again. Let the ocean of the Sangha be clear and pure in this world. The people of the east will be taught and the kalpa will be prolonged. The Proper Dharma will long continue. Such is the meager but genuine resolve I strive to fulfill.

This is the tenth cause and condition for making the resolve to attain Bodhi.

Exhortation

Essay:

Thus we know the ten conditions and are fully aware of the eight aspects. We consequently have a gateway through which to progress and a basis for our development.

We have a human body and live in a favorable country. Our six sense organs are intact and our bodies are healthy. We have complete faith, and fortunately we are without demonic obstacles. Furthermore, we Sanghans have been able to leave the home-life and to receive the complete precepts. We have found a Way Place and have heard the Buddhadharma. We have looked reverently upon the Buddha's sharira and we practice repentance; we have met good friends and are replete with superior conditions. If we fail to make the great resolve today, what are we waiting for?

I hope only that the great assembly will sympathize with my simple-minded sincerity and share my earnest intent. Let us take these vows together. Let us make this resolve together. Whoever has not yet made the resolve should do so now. Whoever has already made the resolve should bolster it. Those who have already bolstered it should continue to advance.

Do not fear difficulty and make a cowardly retreat. Do not consider this matter easy and frivolously waste time. Do not wish for quick results and fail to persevere. Do not become lax and fail in your courage. Do not become dispirited and fail to rouse yourself. Do not let procrastination cause you to delay. Do not let stupidity and dullness keep you from making the resolve. Do not assume that you have shallow roots and are, therefore, unworthy of taking part.

For example, after a tree is planted, the once-shallow roots deepen every day. Similarly, as a knife is sharpened, the blade which was once dull becomes sharp. Because the roots are shallow, would we choose not to plant the tree and allow it to wither away? That the knife is dull is no reason not to sharpen it and to set it aside as useless.

Commentary:

Thus we know the ten conditions, like repaying the Buddha's kindness, our parents' kindness, living beings kindness, the donors' kindness, and causing the Proper Dharma to remain long in the world, **and are fully aware of the eight aspects,** deviant, proper, true, false, great, small, partial, and complete. **We consequently have a gateway through which to progress and a basis for our development,** now we have the land to develop and build on.

We all **have a human body and live in a favorable country. Our six sense organs are intact and our bodies are healthy.** Our eyes, ears, noses, tongues, bodies, and minds, the six sense faculties, are all complete and functioning properly. **We have complete faith** in the Buddha's teaching, **and fortunately we are without demonic obstacles. Furthermore, we Sanghans,** the monastics from whom Great Master Sying An wrote this essay for, **have been able to leave the home-life, and to receive the complete precepts,** the ten precepts of a Shramanera, the two hundred fifty Bhikshu precepts, and the ten major and forty-eight minor Bodhisattva precepts.

We have found a Way Place, a good place to cultivate, **and have heard** and learned to understand **the Buddhadharma. We**

have looked reverently upon and bowed to **the Buddha's sharira and we practice repentance; we have met** so many **good friends and are replete with superior conditions. If we fail to make the great** Bodhi **resolve today, what are we waiting for?**

I hope only that the great assembly will sympathize with my simple-minded sincerity and share my earnest intent, my simple way of thinking. **Let us take these** forty-eight **vows together. Let us make this resolve,** based on the ten reasons to resolve our minds, **together. Whoever has not yet made the resolve should do so now.** Do it now. **Whoever has already made the resolve should bolster it.** Help it along. **Those who have already bolstered it should continue to advance.** Advance without retreating from your resolve to reach Bodhi!

Do not fear the **difficulty** involved in cultivating the Bodhisattva path **and make a cowardly retreat. Do not consider this matter** of resolving on Bodhi **easy and frivolously waste time,** and not pay attention. **Do not wish for quick results and fail to persevere.** There is a saying, "Charge forward too fast and you'll retreat just as fast." Don't be greedy for speed. It is easy to rush forward on a burst of enthusiasm, but it is hard to advance daily at a regulated pace for a long time. We must see things through, and not stop until we reach the goals we set for ourselves. We must be responsible in what we do, and never shirk our duties. We must not retreat from our resolve to reach Bodhi. **Do not become lax and fail in your courage.** Don't hanker to take a break. **Do not become dispirited** and groggy or listless **and fail to rouse yourself. Do not let procrastination cause you to delay.** "Wait a while," you say, "We don't need to recite sutras today, we can recite more tomorrow to make up for it." Procrastinators have many reasons for putting things off. But then can they skip sleep tonight and sleep a bit more tomorrow night? Can they fast today and eat a bit more tomorrow? Well, if they cannot procrastinate about eating, sleeping, and dressing, they shouldn't put off cultivating either.

Do not let stupidity and dullness keep you from making the resolve. Don't think you are dumb and muddled, and unable to make the resolve. **Do not assume that you have shallow roots and are, therefore, unworthy of taking part** in resolving on Bodhi.

For example, after a tree is planted, the once-shallow roots deepen every day. Similarly, as a knife is sharpened, the once-dull blade becomes sharp. If you never grind a dull blade, it will always be dull; whet it and it will be sharp. Simply **because the roots are shallow, would we choose not to plant the tree and allow it to wither away? That the knife is dull is no reason not to sharpen it and to set it aside as useless.** Work with it!

78

Conclusion

Essay:

Moreover, if we feel that cultivation makes us suffer, it is because we do not know that laxity will make us suffer even more. Cultivation entails a brief period of diligent toil, but it yields peace and joy for kalpas without end. One lifetime of laxity and of shirking work results in suffering for many lifetimes to come.

Furthermore, with the Pure Land as our ship, what fear is there that we will retreat? Once we attain the power of patience with the non-existence of beings and phenomena, what difficulty can trouble us? When we know that in past kalpas there were even offenders in the hells who were able to resolve themselves upon Bodhi, how can we human disciples of the Buddha fail to make great vows in this life?

Since time without beginning, we have been muddled and confused. It is useless to remonstrate with ourselves about the past, but we can wake up now, and begin immediately to make amends.

Since we are confused and not yet enlightened, we are certainly to be pitied. But if we know that we should cultivate yet we fail to practice, we are especially pathetic. If we fear the suffering in the hells, we will naturally be vigorous. If we remember the imminence of death, we will not become lazy. Moreover, we must take the Buddhadharma as our whip and find good friends to urge us on. For this short time, do not leave them. Rely on them to the end of your life. Then you need not fear retreat.

Do not say that one thought is a small matter. Do not feel that vows are empty and useless. If our resolves are true, then we can realize our goals. When our vows are vast in scope, then our practice will go deep. Empty space is not big, but the ultimate resolve is gigantic. Vajra is not durable, but vow-power is supremely durable.

Great assembly! If indeed you can accept my words, then from now on, all pledge fraternity in the retinue of Bodhi and sign a compact of kinship in a lotus society. We vow to be reborn together in the Pure Land, to see Amitabha Buddha together, to transform living beings together, and to attain Right Enlightenment together.

How do we know that our future perfection of the thirty-two hallmarks and the hundred blessings' adornments does not begin on this day that we make this resolve and set our vows? I hope that the members of the great assembly will urge each other on. What good fortune! How lucky we are!

Commentary:

Moreover, if we feel that cultivation makes us suffer, being vegetarian, not doing this, not doing that; it is very restrictive. But **it is because we do not know that laxity will make us suffer even more. Cultivation entails a brief period of diligent toil,** for a short while you refrain from excessive creature comforts. **But it yields peace and joy for kalpas without end. One lifetime of laxity and of shirking work results in suffering for many lifetimes to come.** You'll never get out of the sea of suffering. You might feel comfortable for brief moments, thinking you are living it up with good meals or a nice home, but it is all temporary and won't last. You can fall into the hells, become a hungry ghost, or become an animal. But if you cultivate to success, you will be reborn in the Pure Land and will be happy forever.

Furthermore, with the Pure Land as our ship, to sail us out of the sea of suffering, **what fear** or worry **is there that we will retreat** or suffer? **Once we attain the power of patience with the non-existence of beings and phenomena, what difficulty can trouble us?** Nothing will be unbearably painful, and we won't need to seek happiness; thus, with the patience with the non-existence of beings and phenomena, we won't see pain or delight, coming into being or ceasing to be. **When we know that in past kalpas there were even offenders in the hells who were able to resolve themselves upon Bodhi,** that those beings in the hells got out quickly once they resolved to attain Bodhi. **How can we human disciples of the Buddha fail to make great vows in this life?**

Since time without beginning, we have been muddled and confused. From many kalpas past, we have been ignorant and muddled, but **it is useless to remonstrate with ourselves about the past.** The past is gone, we have no way to change it, **but we can wake up now, and begin immediately to make amends.** We still can make up for the past and redeem ourselves.

Since we are confused and not yet enlightened, we are certainly to be pitied. But if we know that we should cultivate yet we fail to practice, if we know we should make vows but fail to do so, **we are especially pathetic. If we fear the suffering in the hells, we will naturally be vigorous. If we remember the imminence of death,** the ghost of impermanence comes for you quickly, **we will not become lazy. Moreover, we must take the Buddhadharma as our whip and find good friends to urge us on. For this short time, do not leave them** or the Dharma. **Rely on them** and the Dharma, **to the end of your life. Then you need not fear retreat.**

Do not say that one thought is a small matter. Do not feel that vows are empty and useless. If our resolves and vows **are**

true, then we can realize our goals. **When our vows are vast in scope, then our practice will go deep** and advance. **Empty space is not big, but the ultimate resolve is gigantic;** it is measureless. **Vajra,** the hardest thing in this world, **is not** as **durable** as your **vow-power, which, if you never forget your vows, is supremely durable.**

Great assembly! If indeed you can accept my words and resolve not to forget them **then from now on, all pledge fraternity in the retinue of Bodhi,** we'll be together, and **sign a compact of kinship in a lotus society. We vow to be reborn together in the Pure Land, to see Amitabba Buddha together,** and then **to transform living beings together, and to attain Right Enlighten- ment,** becoming Buddhas, **together.**

How do we know that our future perfection of the thirty-two hallmarks and the hundred blessings' adornments of the hundred blessings does not begin on this day that we make our resolve on Bodhi **and set our vows?** Our future success starts today. **I hope that the members of the great assembly will urge each other on.** Make good vows and follow them. **What good fortune! How lucky we are!** We are really fortunate!

Glossary

This glossary is an aid for readers unfamiliar with the Buddhist vocabuluary. Definitions have been kept simple, and are not necessarily complete.

Amitabha Buddha
The Buddha of the Western Land of Ultimate Bliss.

Arhat
An enlightened sage of the Small Vehicle.

Asamkhyeya kalpas
An uncountable period of time.

Bhikshu
A fully ordained Buddhist monk, one who leads a pure and celibate life and upholds 250 precepts.

Bhikshuni
A fully ordained Buddhist nun, one who leads a pure and celibate life and upholds 348 precepts.

Bodhi
Enlightenment.

Bodhisattva
An enlightened being who does not enter Nirvana but chooses instead to remain in the world and save living beings.

Buddhadharma
Methods of cultivation taught by the Buddha leading beings to enlightenment.

Buddha
The Enlightened One; one who has reached the Utmost, Right and Equal Enlightenment.

Chan school
One of the five major schools of Buddhism. The teaching of medi-

tation. (Sanskrit: Dhyana; Japansese: Zen)

Confucius

The foremost sage and philosopher of China who lived in the fifth century B.C., he taught that every person should fulfill his or her proper role in family and society. Hs philosophy forms the basis for much of the classic Chinese culture and tradition.

Cultivation

The practical application of the methods taught by the Buddha that leads to enlightenment. Such spiritual practice is likened to the process of cultivating a field, starting from plowing and planting and resulting in fruition, harvest, and storage.

Dedication plaques

Symbols of support for the living and the dead in the form of temporary or permanent memorials.

Dharma

The teachings of the Buddha. After the Buddha's Nirvana, the Dharma passes through the following historical periods:

1. The first 1,000 years is the Proper Dharma Age.
2. The following 1,000 years is the Dharma Image Age.
3. The following 10,000 years is the Dharma-ending Age.

Dharma Appearances School

Dharma Appearances School discussed existence.

Dharma-door

An entrance to the Dharma, a method of practice leading to enlightenment.

Dharma Nature School

Dharma Nature School discussed emptiness.

Dharma Realm

The enlightened world, that is, the totality or infinity of the realm of the Buddhas; a particular plane of existence, as in the Ten Dharma Realms.

Expedient means

Skillful methods used by wise mentors to help teach living beings.

The methods range from admonishing to encouraging.

Externalist

Follower of a heterodox sect.

Five precepts

The five lay precepts are: no killing, no stealing, no sexual misconduct, no false speech, and no intoxicants.

Four-fold assembly

The ordained and novice monks and nuns are the two assemblies. The male and femaled lay community are added to make four.

Fully-ordained monastics

See Bhikshu and Bhikshuni.

Good and Wise Advisor

Someone with knowledge, wisdom, and experience; a wise counsel, spiritual guide, or honest and pure friend in cultivation.

Good roots

The result of good deeds done in any given lifetime, good roots accumulate and provide a foundation upon which practitioners rely and which they continue to build each life.

Great Vehicle

The Mahayana tradition, which bases itself on the resolve for Bodhi and on vows to save living beings.

Hells

One of the six paths of rebirth, the hells are created by beings' karmic mistakes. Beings undergo retribution for those mistakes in hells of their own making and when the retribution is complete, beings are reborn in others paths.

Kalpa

Eon. There are small, medium, and large kalpas, with twenty small equalling one medium and four medium equalling one large.

Karma

Deeds, activity. Karma does not mean fate. It means the deeds which we create ouselves and the retributions which those deeds bring upon us.

Lay people

Two of the four-fold assembly, these men and women are house-holders or single practitioners who have taken refuge with the Triple Jewel.

Land of Ultimate Bliss

The Buddhaland of Amitabha Buddha in the West created through the power of his vows, which enable living beings to be reborn simply by sincere mindfulness and recitation of his name. Also known as the Western Pure Land.

Leave home

To renounce the householder's life and become a monk or nun in order to devote oneself completely to the practice of the Buddhad-harma.

Merit and virtue

Not being separated from our own nature is merit; the correct use of the nature is virtue. Inner humility is merit; showing sincere outer reverence is virtue. We amass merit and virtue through good deeds and good character.

Monastics

Refers to people who have left the home life to become Buddhist monks and nuns. See Bhikshu, Bhikshuni.

Nirvana

Perfect quiescence realized by enlightened sages.

Outflows

All bad habits and faults are outflows. Outflows are the root of birth and death; they let our vital energy leak away.

Pure Land

See Land of Ultimate Bliss.

Repentance ceremonies

Rituals performed alone or in groups that help purify our natures, rid us of karmic obstructions, and allow us to dedicate merit and virtue to others.

Samadhi

A wholesome state of concentration gained through meditation and other practices; there are various kinds of samadhi.

Sangha

The community of Buddhist monks and nuns.

Sanghan

A member of the Sangha; a monk or nun.

Seven Buddhas of Antiquity

They are Vipashyin, Shikhin, Vishvabhu, who belong to the previous Adornment kalpa, and Krakucchanda, Kanakamuni, Kashyapa, and Shakyamuni, who belong to the present Worthy kalpa.

Sharira

Jewel-like relics found upon cremation, which indicate control of outflows that comes with pure practice.

Shastras

Commentaries on the teachings of the Buddha spoken by Buddhist Patriarchs and disciples of the Buddha.

Six Guiding Principles of the City of Ten Thousand Buddhas

Refraining from fighting, greed, seeking personal gain, selfishness, pursuing advantages, and lying.

six spiritual powers

The heavenly eye, heavenly ear, knowledge of previous lives, knowledge of the minds of others, complete spirit, and ending of outflows.

Spiritual nature

The Buddha nature inherent in us all. Also referred to as the self-nature. All beings are endowed with this nature; all have the potential to become fully enlightened.

Stupa

Reliquaries designed to hold the remains of Buddhas, Buddhist saints, and founders and leaders of lineages.

Sutra
Discourses by the Buddha or by various members of the assembly with the authority of the Buddha.

Ten Major and Forth-eight Minor Bodhisattva Precepts
Found in the Brahma Net Sutra, these precepts are the foundation of the Mahayana vinaya.

Ten Precepts
The precepts held by novice monks and nuns, known as shramaneras and shramanerikas.

Theravada Buddhism
The southern transmission of Buddhism, found primarily in Sri Lanka, Burma, Thailand, and other countries of Southeast Asia.

Tripitaka
The "Three Treasuries", the Buddhist Canon, which is divided into three divisions – Sutras, Vinayas and Shastras.

Triple Jewel
The Buddha, the Dharma and the Sangha.

Triple Realm
Refers to the three realms: Desire Realm, in which we live; the Form Realm, heavens free of desire that are reached through meditation and cultivation or rebirth; and the Formless Realm; heavens free of desire and form that are reached through meditation and cultivation or rebirth.

Turning wheel
Cycle of transmigration in the six paths.

Upasaka/Upasika
A Buddhist layman/laywoman who has taken refuge with the Triple Jewel.

Vajra
A Sanskrit word which means "durable," "luminous," and "able to cut." It is indestructible and is usually represented by diamond.

Vajra Light Jeweled Precept Substance
A term for the intangible substance of the precepts.

Vinaya (moral precepts)

The collected moral regulations governing the life of the Buddhist monastic community, one of the three divisions of the Buddhist canon. The Vinaya includes all the precept-regulations, methods we use to keep watch over ourselves so that it is not necessary for anyone else to keep an eye on us.

The Way

The spiritual path of cultivation; the ultimate truth, which is realized through following that path.

Yin and Yang

Yin is the female principle, usually depicted as the dark, negative element; yang is the male principle, usually depicted as the light, positive element. At the level of relativity, these two are interdependent and compliment each other.

The pure yang ascribed to Buddhas transcends the dual aspects of ordinary yin and yang.

General Index

Buddhist Text Translation Society Publication

Buddhist Text Translation Society
International Translation Institute

http://www.bttsonline.org

1777 Murchison Drive,
Burlingame, California 94010-4504 USA
Phone: 650-692-5912 Fax: 650-692-5056

When Buddhism first came to China from India, one of the most important tasks required for its establishment was the translation of the Buddhist scriptures from Sanskrit into Chinese. This work involved a great many people, such as the renowned monk National Master Kumarajiva (fifth century), who led an assembly of over 800 people to work on the translation of the Tripitaka (Buddhist canon) for over a decade. Because of the work of individuals such as these, nearly the entire Buddhist Tripitaka of over a thousand texts exists to the present day in Chinese.

Now the banner of the Buddha's Teachings is being firmly planted in Western soil, and the same translation work is being done from Chinese into English. Since 1970, the Buddhist Text Translation Society (BTTS) has been making a paramount contribution toward this goal. Aware that the Buddhist Tripitaka is a work of such magnitude that its translation could never be entrusted to a single person, the BTTS, emulating the translation assemblies of ancient times, does not publish a work until it has passed through four committees for primary translation, revision, editing, and certification. The leaders of these committees are Bhikshus (monks) and Bhikshunis (nuns) who have devoted their lives to the study and practice of the Buddha's teachings. For this reason, all of the works of the BTTS put an emphasis on what the principles of the Buddha's teachings mean in terms of actual practice and not simply hypothetical conjecture.

The translations of canonical works by the Buddhist Text Translation Society are accompanied by extensive commentaries by the Venerable Tripitaka Master Hsuan Hua.

BTTS Publications

Buddhist Sutras. Amitabha Sutra, Dharma Flower (Lotus) Sutra, Flower Adornment (Avatamsaka) Sutra, Heart Sutra & Verses without a Stand, Shurangama Sutra, Sixth Patriarch Sutra, Sutra in Forty-two Sections, Sutra of the Past Vows of Earth Store Bodhisattva, Vajra Prajna Paramita (Diamond) Sutra.

Commentarial Literature. Buddha Root Farm, City of 10 000 Buddhas Recitation Handbook, Filiality: The Human Source, Herein Lies the Treasure-trove, Listen to Yourself Think Everything Over, Shastra on the Door to Understanding the Hundred Dharmas, Song of Enlightenment, The Ten Dharma Realms Are Not Beyond a Single Thought, Venerable Master Hua's Talks on Dharma, Venerable Master Hua's Talks on Dharma during the 1993 Trip to Taiwan, Water Mirror Reflecting Heaven.

Biographical. In Memory of the Venerable Master Hsuan Hua, Pictorial Biography of the Venerable Master Hsü Yün, Records of High Sanghans, Records of the Life of the Venerable Master Hsüan Hua, Three Steps One Bow, World Peace Gathering, News from True Cultivators, Open Your Eyes Take a Look at the World, With One Heart Bowing to the City of 10 000 Buddhas.

Children's Books. Cherishing Life, Human Roots: Buddhist Stories for Young Readers, Spider Web, Giant Turtle, Patriarch Bodhidharma.

Musics, Novels and Brochures. Songs for Awakening, Awakening, The Three Cart Patriarch, City of 10 000 Buddhas Color Brochure, Celebrisi's Journey, Lots of Time Left.

The Buddhist Monthly–Vajra Bodhi Sea is a monthly journal of orthodox Buddhism which has been published by the Dharma Realm Buddhist Association, formerly known as the Sino-American Buddhist Association, since 1970. Each issue contains the most recent translations of the Buddhist canon by the Buddhist Text Translation Society. Also included in each issue are a biography of a great Patriarch of Buddhism from the ancient past, sketches of the lives of contemporary monastics and lay-followers around the world, articles on practice, and other material. The journal is bilingual, Chinese and English

Please visit our web-site at **www.bttsonline.org** for the latest publications and for ordering information.

The Dharma Realm Buddhist Association

Mission

The Dharma Realm Buddhist Association (formerly the Sino-American Buddhist Association) was founded by the Venerable Master Hsuan Hua in the United States of America in 1959. Taking the Dharma Realm as its scope, the Association aims to disseminate the genuine teachings of the Buddha throughout the world. The Association is dedicated to translating the Buddhist canon, propagating the Orthodox Dharma, promoting ethical education, and bringing benefit and happiness to all beings. Its hope is that individuals, families, the society, the nation, and the entire world will, under the transforming influence of the Buddhadharma, gradually reach the state of ultimate truth and goodness.

The Founder

The Venerable Master, whose names were An Tse and To Lun, received the Dharma name Hsuan Hua and the transmission of Dharma from Venerable Master Hsu Yun in the lineage of the Wei Yang Sect. He was born in Manchuria, China, at the beginning of the century. At nineteen, he entered the monastic order and dwelt in a hut by his mother's grave to practice filial piety. He meditated, studied the teachings, ate only one meal a day, and slept sitting up. In 1948 he went to Hong Kong, where he established the Buddhist Lecture Hall and other Way-places. In 1962 he brought the Proper Dharma to the West, lecturing on several dozen Mahayana Sutras in the United States. Over the years, the Master established more than twenty monasteries of Proper Dharma under the auspices of the Dharma Realm Buddhist Association and the City of Ten Thousand Buddhas. He also founded centers for the translation of the Buddhist canon and for education to spread the influence of the Dharma in the East and West. The Master manifested the stillness in the United States in 1995. Through his lifelong, selfless dedication to teaching living beings with wisdom and compassion, he influenced countless people to change their faults and to walk upon the pure, bright path to enlightenment.

Dharma Propagation, Buddhist Text Translation, and Education

The Venerable Master Hua's three great vows after leaving the home-life were (1) to propagate the Dharma, (2) to translate the Buddhist Canon, and (3) to promote education. In order to make these vows a reality, the Venerable Master based himself on the Three Principles and the Six Guidelines. Courageously facing every hardship, he founded monasteries, schools, and centers in the West, drawing in living beings and teaching them on a vast scale. Over the years, he founded the following institutions:

The City of Ten Thousand Buddhas and Its Branches

In propagating the Proper Dharma, the Venerable Master not only trained people but also founded Way-places where the Dharma wheel could turn and living beings could be saved. He wanted to provide cultivators with pure places to practice in accord with the Buddha's regulations. Over the years, he founded many Way-places of Proper Dharma. In the United States and Canada, these include the City of Ten Thousand Buddhas; Gold Mountain Monastery; Gold Sage Monastery; Gold Wheel Monastery; Gold Summit Monastery; Gold Buddha Monastery; Avatamsaka Monastery; Long Beach Monastery; the City of the Dharma Realm; Berkeley Buddhist Monastery; Avatamsaka Hermitage; and Blessings, Prosperity, and Longevity Monastery. In Taiwan, there are the Dharma Realm Buddhist Books Distribution Association, Dharma Realm Monastery, and Amitabha Monastery. In Malaysia, there are the Prajna Guanyin Sagely Monastery (formerly Tze Yun Tung Temple), Deng Bi An Monastery, and Lotus Vihara. In Hong Kong, there are the Buddhist Lecture Hall and Cixing Monastery.

Purchased in 1974, the City of Ten Thousand Buddhas is the hub of the Dharma Realm Buddhist Association. The City is located in Talmage, Mendocino County, California, 110 miles north of San Francisco. Eighty of the 488 acres of land are in active use. The remaining acreage consists of meadows, orchards, and woods. With over seventy large buildings containing over 2,000 rooms, blessed with serenity and fresh, clean air, it is the first large Buddhist monastic community in the United States. It is also an international center for the Proper Dharma.

Although the Venerable Master Hua was the Ninth Patriarch in the Wei Yang Sect of the Chan School, the monasteries he founded emphasize all of the five main practices of Mahayana Buddhism (Chan meditation, Pure Land, esoteric, Vinaya (moral discipline), and doctrinal studies). This accords with the Buddha's words: "The Dharma is level and equal, with no high or low." At the City of Ten Thousand Buddhas, the rules of purity are rigorously observed. Residents of the City strive to regulate their own conduct and to cultivate with vigor. Taking refuge in the Proper Dharma, they lead pure and selfless lives, and attain peace in body and mind. The Sutras are expounded and the Dharma wheel is turned daily. Residents dedicate themselves wholeheartedly to making Buddhism flourish. Monks and nuns in all the monasteries take one meal a day, always wear their precept sash, and follow the Three Principles:

> *Freezing, we do not scheme.*
> *Starving, we do not beg.*
> *Dying of poverty, we ask for nothing.*
> *According with conditions, we do not change.*
> *Not changing, we accord with conditions.*
> *We adhere firmly to our three great principles.*
> *We renounce our lives to do the Buddha's work.*
> *We take the responsibility to mold our own destinies.*
> *We rectify our lives to fulfill the Sanghan's role.*
> *Encountering specific matters,*
>   *we understand the principles.*
> *Understanding the principles,*
>   *we apply them in specific matters.*
> *We carry on the single pulse of*
>   *the Patriarchs' mind-transmission.*

The monasteries also follow the Six Guidelines: not contending, not being greedy, not seeking, not being selfish, not pursuing personal advantage, and not lying.

International Translation Institute

The Venerable Master vowed to translate the Buddhist Canon (Tripitaka) into Western languages so that it would be widely accessible throughout the world. In 1973, he founded the International Translation Institute on Washington Street in San Francisco for the purpose of translating Buddhist scriptures into English and other languages. In 1977, the Institute was merged into Dharma Realm Buddhist University as the Institute for the Translation of Buddhist Texts. In 1991, the Venerable Master purchased a large building in Burlingame (south of San Francisco) and established the International Translation Institute there for the purpose of translating and publishing Buddhist texts. To date, in addition to publishing over one hundred volumes of Buddhist texts in Chinese, the Association has published more than one hundred volumes of English, French, Spanish, Vietnamese, and Japanese translations of Buddhist texts, as well as bilingual (Chinese and English) editions. Audio and video tapes also continue to be produced. The monthly journal Vajra Bodhi Sea, which has been in circulation for nearly thirty years, has been published in bilingual (Chinese and English) format in recent years.

In the past, the difficult and vast mission of translating the Buddhist canon in China was sponsored and supported by the emperors and kings themselves. In our time, the Venerable Master encouraged his disciples to cooperatively shoulder this heavy responsibility, producing books and audio tapes and using the medium of language to turn the wheel of Proper Dharma and do the great work of the Buddha. All those who aspire to devote themselves to this work of sages should uphold the Eight Guidelines of the International Translation Institute:

1. One must free oneself from the motives of personal fame and profit.
2. One must cultivate a respectful and sincere attitude free from arrogance and conceit.
3. One must refrain from aggrandizing one's work and denigrating that of others.
4. One must not establish oneself as the standard of correctness and suppress the work of others with one's fault-finding.
5. One must take the Buddha-mind as one's own mind.
6. One must use the wisdom of Dharma-Selecting Vision to determine true principles.
7. One must request Virtuous Elders of the ten directions to certify one's translations.
8. One must endeavor to propagate the teachings by printing Sutras, Shastra texts, and Vinaya texts when the translations are certified as being correct.

These are the Venerable Master's vows, and participants in the work of translation should strive to realize them.

Instilling Goodness Elementary School, Developing Virtue Secondary School, Dharma Realm Buddhist University

"Education is the best national defense." The Venerable Master Hua saw clearly that in order to save the world, it is essential to promote good education. If we want to save the world, we have to bring about a complete change in people's minds and guide them to cast out unwholesomeness and to pursue goodness. To this end the Master founded Instilling Goodness Elementary School in 1974, and Developing Virtue Secondary School and Dharma Realm Buddhist University in 1976.

In an education embodying the spirit of Buddhism, the elementary school teaches students to be filial to parents, the secondary school teaches students to be good citizens, and the university teaches such virtues as humaneness and righteousness. Instilling Goodness Elementary School and Developing Virtue Secondary School combine the best of contemporary and traditional methods and of Western and Eastern cultures. They emphasize moral virtue and spiritual development, and aim to guide students to become good and capable citizens who will benefit humankind. The schools offer a bilingual (Chinese/English) program where boys and girls study separately. In addition to standard academic courses, the curriculum includes ethics, meditation, Buddhist studies, and so on, giving students a foundation in virtue and guiding them to understand themselves and explore the truths of the universe. Branches of the schools (Sunday schools) have been established at branch monasteries with the aim of propagating filial piety and ethical education.

Dharma Realm Buddhist University, whose curriculum focuses on the Proper Dharma, does not merely transmit academic knowledge. It emphasizes a foundation in virtue, which expands into the study of how to help all living beings discover their inherent nature. Thus, Dharma Realm Buddhist University advocates a spirit of shared inquiry and free exchange of ideas, encouraging students to study various canonical texts and use different experiences and learning styles to tap their inherent wisdom and fathom the meanings of those texts. Students are encouraged to practice the principles they have understood and apply the Buddhadharma in their lives, thereby nurturing their wisdom and virtue. The University aims to produce outstanding individuals of high moral character who will be able to bring benefit to all sentient beings.

Sangha and Laity Training Programs

In the Dharma-ending Age, in both Eastern and Western societies there are very few monasteries that actually practice the Buddha's regulations and strictly uphold the precepts. Teachers with genuine wisdom and understanding, capable of guiding those who aspire to pursue careers in Buddhism, are very rare. The Venerable Master founded the Sangha and Laity Training Programs in 1982 with the goals of raising the caliber of the Sangha, perpetuating the Proper Dharma, providing professional training for Buddhists around the world on both practical and theoretical levels, and transmitting the wisdom of the Buddha.

The Sangha Training Program gives monastics a solid foundation in Buddhist studies and practice, training them in the practical affairs of Buddhism and Sangha management. After graduation, students will be able to assume various responsibilities related to Buddhism in monasteries, institutions, and other settings. The program emphasizes a thorough knowledge of Buddhism, understanding of the scriptures, earnest cultivation, strict observance of precepts, and the development of a virtuous character, so that students will be able to propagate the Proper Dharma and perpetuate the Buddha's wisdom. The Laity Training Program offers courses to help laypeople develop correct views, study and practice the teachings, and understand monastic regulations and ceremonies, so that they will be able to contribute their abilities in Buddhist organizations.

Let Us Go Forward Together

In this Dharma-ending Age when the world is becoming increasingly dangerous and evil, the Dharma Realm Buddhist Association, in consonance with its guiding principles, opens the doors of its monasteries and centers to those of all religions and nationalities. Anyone who is devoted to humaneness, righteousness, virtue, and the pursuit of truth, and who wishes to understand him or herself and help humankind, is welcome to come study and practice with us. May we together bring benefit and happiness to all living beings.

Dharma Realm Buddhist Association Branches

The City of Ten Thousand Buddhas
P.O. Box 217, Talmage, CA 95481-0217 USA
Tel: (707) 462-0939 Fax: (707) 462-0949
Home Page: **http://www.drba.org**

Institute for World Religions (Berkeley Buddhist Monastery)
2304 McKinley Avenue, Berkeley, CA 94703 USA
Tel: (510) 848-3440

Dharma Realm Buddhist Books Distribution Society
11th Floor, 85 Chung-hsiao E. Road, Sec. 6, Taipei, Taiwan R.O.C.
Tel: (02) 2786-3022 Fax: (02) 2786-2674

The City of the Dharma Realm
1029 West Capitol Avenue, West Sacramento, CA 95691 USA
Tel: (916) 374-8268

Gold Mountain Monastery
800 Sacramento Street, San Francisco, CA 94108 USA
Tel: (415) 421-6117 Fax: (415) 788-6001

Gold Wheel Monastery
235 North Avenue 58, Los Angeles, CA 90042 USA
Tel: (323) 258-6668

Gold Buddha Monastery
248 East 11th Avenue, Vancouver, B.C. V5T 2C3 Canada
Tel: (604) 709-0248 Fax: (604) 684-3754

Gold Summit Monastery
233 1st Avenue, West Seattle, WA 98119 USA
Tel: (206) 284-6690 Fax: (206) 284-6918

Gold Sage Monastery
11455 Clayton Road, San Jose, CA 95127 USA
Tel: (408) 923-7243 Fax: (408) 923-1064

The International Translation Institute
1777 Murchison Drive, Burlingame, CA 94010-4504 USA
Tel: (650) 692-5912 Fax: (650) 692-5056

Long Beach Monastery
3361 East Ocean Boulevard, Long Beach, CA 90803 USA
Tel: (562) 438-8902

Blessings, Prosperity, & Longevity Monastery
4140 Long Beach Boulevard, Long Beach, CA 90807 USA
Tel: (562) 595-4966

Avatamsaka Hermitage
11721 Beall Mountain Road, Potomac, MD 20854-1128 USA
Tel: (301) 299-3693

Avatamsaka Monastery
1009 4th Avenue, S.W. Calgary, AB T2P OK8 Canada
Tel: (403) 234-0644

Kun Yam Thong Temple
161, Jalan Ampang, 50450 Kuala Lumpur, Malaysia
Tel: (03) 2164-8055 Fax: (03) 2163-7118

Prajna Guanyin Sagely Monastery (formerly Tze Yun Tung)
Batu 5½, Jalan Sungai Besi,
Salak Selatan, 57100 Kuala Lumpur, Malaysia
Tel: (03) 7982-6560 Fax: (03) 7980-1272

Lotus Vihara
136, Jalan Sekolah, 45600 Batang Berjuntai,
Selangor Darul Ehsan, Malaysia
Tel: (03) 3271-9439

Buddhist Lecture Hall
31 Wong Nei Chong Road, Top Floor, Happy Valley, Hong Kong, China
Tel: (02) 2572-7644

Dharma Realm Sagely Monastery
20, Tong-hsi Shan-chuang, Hsing-lung Village, Liu-kuei
Kaohsiung County, Taiwan, R.O.C.
Tel: (07) 689-3717 Fax: (07) 689-3870

Amitabha Monastery
7, Su-chien-hui, Chih-nan Village, Shou-feng,
Hualien County, Taiwan, R.O.C.
Tel: (07) 865-1956 Fax: (07) 865-3426

Verse of Transference

May the merit and virtue accrued from this work,
Adorn the Buddhas' Pure Lands,
Repaying four kinds of kindness above,
And aiding those suffering in the paths below.

May those who see and hear of this,
All bring forth the resolve for Bodhi,
And when this retribution body is over,
Be born together in the Land of Ultimate Bliss.

Dharma Protector Wei Tuo Bodhisattva